STORM AND PEACE

WILLIAM CAVENDISH, THIRD DUKE OF DEVONSHIRE

From the Portrait by Sir Joshua Reynolds at Chatsworth.

STORM AND PEACE

JOHN BERESFORD

Essay Index Reprint Series

BOOKS FOR LIBRARIES PRESS, INC.
FREEPORT, NEW YORK

First Published 1936
Reprinted 1967

LIBRARY OF CONGRESS CATALOG CARD NUMBER:
67-28744

PRINTED IN THE UNITED STATES OF AMERICA

DEDICATION

To the Memory
of
My Father and Mother:

John Jervis Beresford, M.A., sometime Rector of Easton Grey, Wilts, and Margaret Moreton Hollinsed, his wife, who brought up their children in the love of literature, and having endured the tempests of life, entered (she in the year 1915, he in the year 1916) the Peace of God.

CONTENTS

INTRODUCTION

The longest essay—*The Crisis of 1745*—and that on General Gordon explain the first word of the title of this book.

I am deeply indebted to the Duke of Devonshire for permission to make such full use of the Chatsworth MSS. on which the essay on the '45 is based. Very little of this material, so rich in historical and human interest, has been printed before.[1] It is now some ten years since I first visited Chatsworth and examined the MSS. In the summer of 1933 I again took up the task—which I had been compelled to lay aside for a variety of reasons—and I offer this essay as a study in the human side of history, the side which has always interested me most, setting me on to *Gossip of the Seventeenth and Eighteenth Centuries*, and in search of Parson Woodforde, Mr. Du Quesne and other friends long dead and gone.

In storm Gordon—to turn to him for a moment—passed almost his entire life. Moreover, as we become acquainted with his career, he has the power of conveying a sense of agitation. So much is this the case that when some eight years ago I began to read his *Letters to his Sister* I was compelled to lay the book aside for the time being, nor is it

[1] Mr. Eardley Simpson, for his book on *Derby and the Forty-Five* (Philip Allan, 1933), was allowed to inspect the MSS., but he confines himself to quoting some sentences here and there from certain of the documents.

possible to read the letters now without a strange feeling of emotion. The essay is an attempt at critical biography in miniature.

All the remaining essays are concerned with peaceful themes, and the unity of feeling running through them is based on a state of mind which Wordsworth has described better than anyone else in the third book of *The Excursion*:

> *craving peace,*
> *The central feeling of all happiness,*
> *Not as a refuge from distress or pain,*
> *A breathing-time, vacation, or a truce,*
> *But for its absolute self; a life of peace,*
> *Stability without regret or fear;*
> *That hath been, is, and shall be evermore.*

The four principal essays in this book—Nos. 1 to 4—are here published for the first time, together with seven of the shorter ones. I must thank, however, the Editor of *The Times* for permission to reprint Nos. 11, 12 and 13, of *The Times Literary Supplement*, No. 19, of the *Spectator*, Nos. 14 to 18 and No. 22, and of *Country Life*, No. 20.

I wish specially to thank my friend Mr. Francis Thompson, the Librarian of Chatsworth, for all his help when I was examining and copying the Chatsworth MSS.

JOHN BERESFORD

May 1936.

Chapter One

THE CRISIS OF 1745

*Sidelights from Chatsworth on Prince
Charles Edward's Invasion*

The six months from July to December 1745 were as critical as any in the history of England. The flower of her army in Flanders—engaged in the protracted War of the Austrian Succession—had suffered decisive defeat at Fontenoy, and since then the French had been carrying all before them, capturing citadels and towns "as one would gather a nosegay," as Horace Walpole expressed it. Defeat on the Continent, however serious for England's allies, for the Dutch and for Maria Theresa of Austria, would not have mattered so much if it had not involved immediate reactions at home. Here the possibility of a Jacobite Rebellion, which wise old Sir Robert Walpole had always dreaded, was not to be dismissed with George II's light-hearted and incredulous: "Pho! Don't talk to me of that stuff."

On July 23rd old style—one must add on eleven days to get the modern equivalent in new style introduced after 1752—Prince Charles Edward had landed at Eriskay Island. Meanwhile the victorious French were boasting that they could conquer England "with five thousand scullions of the French Army."

The Prime Minister, Henry Pelham, was much discouraged,

not only by the disastrous course of the campaign on
the Continent, but by the intractable character of his
master, George II. For the King at this time hated his Prime
Minister very cordially, and perhaps even more cordially
the Prime Minister's brother, the Duke of Newcastle,
Secretary of State. The Pelhams had secured the dismissal
from office of Lord Granville (better known as Lord
Carteret), but they could not prevent the King from
secretly consulting him, and both the King and Carteret
cared much more for foreign than for domestic affairs.
Certainly it was a consolation to the Pelham brothers to
have the entire support of one of the most sagacious men
who have ever held high office, the great Lord Chancellor
Hardwicke, to enjoy the confidence of the Duke of Cumberland, and to be able to rely on such powerful and sensible
persons as William Cavendish, third Duke of Devonshire,
and his son, Lord Hartington. It was particularly disap-
pointing that affairs on the Continent had taken a turn so
serious as to prevent Henry Pelham, accompanied by his
son-in-law, Lord Lincoln, from journeying down from
London by coach at the end of July to join the Duke of
Devonshire at Hardwick and afterwards at Chatsworth.
And then, as a further cause for irritation, Vincent, the
messenger, had got drunk and lost a most important State
paper containing a full account of foreign affairs despatched
by the Prime Minister to the Duke, had lost it somewhere
near Northampton and had spent much time fruitlessly
looking for it. Altogether everything was intolerably difficult and trying and, "I am to change the most agreeable

party in the world, for a most disagreeable confinement here." He relies much on the Duke's judgement, "shall always be greatly guided by your sentiments" and hopes to see him shortly in London. So ends a letter from the Prime Minister to the Duke of Devonshire dated July 26th, 1745.

Very shortly after this letter had been written ominous reports reached the Prime Minister and his brother, the Duke of Newcastle, that Prince Charles Edward had landed in Scotland. A price was at once set upon the head of the Prince, and Sir John Cope was ordered to assemble the regular troops in Scotland—they numbered only some 2,000. To add to the difficulties of the Pelhams, their principal supporters in Scotland, the great Whig Dukes of Argyll and Athol, deeming discretion the better part of valour, now left their native land and repaired to London. Meanwhile the King, "our master," as Pelham called him, was lingering in his beloved Electorate of Hanover and could not be induced to come back before August 31st. George II returned to find that the Stewart standard had been raised at Glenfinnan, that the clans were rallying to his rival, Prince Charming, that Sir John Cope, unable to risk battle in the Highlands, was making his way back to defend Edinburgh after trudging half round Scotland, and that the Highlanders were on the march. The situation is conveyed in a typically sensible and cool letter from the Duke of Devonshire to his son, the Marquis of Hartington. The Duke had evidently been compelled to return to London from Chatsworth in August: he was not only an influential member of the Government as Lord Steward of the

13

Household, but one of the Lords Justices of the Realm during the absence of the King in Hanover. Only a Cavendish could have written so calm and collected a letter at a time when the principal Ministers were in a state of high agitation. "When I look round me and consider our whole situation," the sober Lord Chancellor Hardwicke said at this time, "our all appears to be at stake." The Duke's letter is dated September 3rd, 1745, and addressed to Lord Hartington at the Right Hon. the Earl of Burlington's, Londesborough, near Market Weighton, Yorkshire.

DEAR Sn [Son]

I was just setting down to answer your Letter by telling you I proposed to be at Chatsworth by Monday next but am sorry I am now obliged to call you away from the Company you are with (to all which I desire my best compliments) for I have just now heard the Rebels who are abt. 2000 & almost all Highlanders and consequently devilish good marchers have slipt by Cope and are marching towards Edingburgh. We have two Regiments of Dragoons abt. Edinburgh wch. I should hope they cannot easily deal with now they are come out of the Highlands, but however we must now take all possible methods to secure ourselves agst. them. I shall not be able to get down sooner, so if you like it you may continue where you are till Monday and I will write to you the best acct. I can by the next Post wch. I suppose you will have by Sunday morning.

I am

Dr. Sn.

Yours etc.

DEVONSHIRE.

William Cavendish, Lord Hartington, afterwards fourth Duke of Devonshire, was at this time twenty-five years of age and a very promising young politician, much regarded by the Pelham brothers. Later on, he was, like his father, Lord Lieutenant of Ireland for a time, and subsequently—from November 1756 to June 1757—he was to become Prime Minister. At the present moment he was engaged in courting Lady Charlotte Boyle, daughter and heiress of Lord Burlington, and great grand-daughter—on her mother's side—of the celebrated Marquis of Halifax. Lady Charlotte was now fourteen, and she married Lord Hartington in March 1748, when she was sixteen and a half; she brought him, as the authors of the *Complete Peerage* observe, "Bolton Abbey and the immense estates of that family in Yorkshire and Derbyshire, as also Chiswick, Burlington House, Piccadilly, and the property in County Cork etc. in Ireland, his political importance being greatly increased by these acquisitions." Lord Hartington was evidently a very charming person, and it was said of him by a contemporary that there was no man so fitted to make a wife happy.

Two days later, on September 5th, the Duke of Devonshire again wrote to his son, giving him the latest news as it was known in London. Admiral Vernon, who was keeping a sharp look out in the Downs, had reported that four French men-of-war and about thirty transports were in Dunkirk. Whereupon the Government—who, it must be remembered, were constantly haunted during these months by just apprehensions of invasion from France—had ordered ten regiments of foot to embark from the army in Flanders, and hasten immediately over to England: "So that I hope we shall soon have them," wrote the Duke, and then, with a sudden transition, betraying no hint of a smile: "I have wrote by this Post to have the Arms at Hardwick cleaned." However, there was good sense in this domestic military precaution, for the Duke continues:

"If the French make any attempt it will probably be in the South: this consideration will occasion the troops to be chiefly quartered to the South of London. So I think we must consider how to keep things quiet in the Northern Counties where there will scarce be any regular troops. Lord Malton [Sir Thomas Wentworth, afterwards created Marquis of Rockingham] has wrote to the Duke of Newcastle [from Yorkshire] to enquire if the Lord Lieutenants can do any thing but in the ordinary way of the Militia. I don't see anything else they can do except they get an Authority from the King to raise companies, troops, or Regiments. Such Authorities have been given formerly. I shall have one but shall not mention it unless I find occasion to make use of it, and shall let Lord Malton know it. As it is not impossible but I may soon be called to London again, I hope you will come and meet me as soon as you can (tho I am very sorry to call you away from the company you are with). I desire you will make my compliments to my Ld. and Lady Burlington and Lady Charlotte, Miss Bedingfield and to Sir Harry and Lady Betty if there. I am most sincerely

Dr. Sn.

Yours etc.

DEVONSHIRE.

If Lord Burlington has no accts. of these things you will communicate these to him."

The Duke of Devonshire shortly after this repaired to his ancestral seat at Chatsworth to concert such measures of local defence as might be necessary. The Pelham brothers kept him constantly in touch with the situation in the wider world. The Prime Minister wrote to him a depressed letter on September 17th, and after expressing the opinion that only regular troops could put a stop to the rebels, proceeds:

"without that, I don't see but they may come into England. But if any force appears against 'em, I am satisfied they will at least disperse; few people come to 'em; their money is pretty near exhausted, and their arms are not of the best."

Then a fresh access of depression comes over Henry Pelham:

"but all our news is uncertain, it comes from different quarters, and is conveyed to us thro very unintelligible hands, for our Secretary of State for that country [the Marquis of Tweeddale, one of the most incompetent Ministers who have ever held office, judging from the correspondence published in Home's *History of the Rebellion*, Vol. III. appendices], in my mind, is never to be understood"

Pelham for his part is far from inattentive to the rebellion, but the attitude of the King is really beyond words, and the Prime Minister lets himself go under the seal of profound secrecy:

Bp

"the conduct of a certain person is worse than ever, to speak of personal treatment is idle at this time, but we are not permitted either to give our advice, or to act in consequence of any advice that is given. . . . In short to you I say it, but under the strictest Eye of secrecy, *I do know that if successors could be found for my Brother and myself* there would be no hesitation in removing us whether we would or no."

The Prime Minister ends his letter by appealing to the Duke to send him his thoughts:

"for I can assure you there is nobody's opinion will have so great weight as your own with him who shall ever desire to subscribe himself, my Dear Lord
Your Grace's most affectionate
and faithfull servt.
H. PELHAM."

It took some days for news from the centre of Scotland to reach London. When Henry Pelham was writing on September 17th, he had heard that the rebels had reached Dunblane. Actually they had reached that place on September 11th; on the 13th they had crossed the Forth, Prince Charles Edward wading through the river at the head of his ferocious and motley host, the half, as Lord Elcho says, completely armed, the others "with pitch forks, scythes, a sword or pistol, or some only a staff or stick." On the 16th they were at the gates of Edinburgh, whose astonished citizens had that day witnessed the panic flight of Gardiner's and Hamilton's dragoons, galloping headlong away from the advancing Highlanders. On the 17th, Edinburgh—all except the Castle—was captured without a shot and the Prince entered Holyrood Palace in triumph. On the memorable September 21st, at three o'clock in the morning, the Highland host overwhelmed Cope's army, which had been advancing to the defence of Edinburgh, at Preston Pans, and won the completest victory in history in the space of eight minutes.

On that very day the Duke of Newcastle wrote to the Duke of Devonshire from Newcastle House in Lincoln's Inn Fields, expressing the hope that Sir John Cope would soon defeat the rebels.

"If the Rebels should march into England, Sir J. Cope has a hint that he is not to understand himself to be restrained by his present Commission from following them hither."

While the Duke was penning these words Sir John Cope —never had fate been in more ironic mood—was flying with the remnant of his cavalry towards the English border, reaching Berwick on the 22nd. News of the disaster did not reach London until the 24th.

"It is a matter of the greatest Amazement," wrote the Duke of Newcastle in the letter just cited, in commentary on the capture of Edinburgh, "and will hereafter hardly be credited that a Parcel of Rebel Highlanders, at first so inconsiderable in their Numbers, should be able to go through the greatest Part of Scotland; and possess themselves of the Capital of that Kingdom, without Opposition."

He was so taken aback when the news of Preston Pans arrived that he wrote two letters to the Duke of Devonshire from Whitehall on September 25th, the one just conveying

"the melancholy account we had yesterday morning of the defeat of His Majesty's Forces . . . by the Rebels in Scotland,"

the other in more resilient mood as follows:

MY LORD

I am persuaded it will be agreeable to your Grace to be informed, that a Body of Troops amounting in the whole to near Ten Thousand Men, with a sufficient Train of Artillery etc., under the Command of Marshall Wade, will immediately march Northwards, in pursuit of the Rebels wherever they are, His Majesty being determined by the Blessing of God, to do his utmost immediately and Effectually to suppress this Rebellion, to protect his faithfull subjects, and to relieve and defend the several Counties, which lie most exposed to the Insults and attacks of this lawless and rebellious Multitude.

I am etc.,

HOLLES NEWCASTLE.

There was something about the mere thought of the Scots which excited Englishmen at this time to a frenzy of indignation. We wish we could have overheard the Duke of Devonshire's comments when he opened the Duke of Newcastle's letter conveying news of the defeat of Preston Pans. Doubtless his sentiments corresponded with those recorded in the letter of a Lieutenant Robinson printed in Philip Yorke's exhaustive *Life of Lord Chancellor Hardwicke*:

"When you have nothing to do," wrote Lieutenant Robinson to a brother officer, "pray employ your time meritoriously, as I do, in damning, sinking, confounding the whole Scotch nation."

The Duke of Devonshire, whose admirable portrait by Reynolds conveys the impression of a person of solid sense, portly and tranquil, was determined to play his part in rousing the loyal men of Derbyshire. His very house, begun by his grandfather, the first Duke, in the year 1687, and finished in four-square Palladian splendour early in the reign of Queen Anne, was, in effect, a permanent memorial of what the Revolution had meant. And now the grandson of King James II was challenging the existence of all that the Duke's ancestors had stood for—freedom from arbitrary government, and religious liberty, and, above all, enduring English tranquillity. For Chatsworth, even beyond the other great houses of England, conveys at once a sense of calm, of solemn magnificence, of what man can accomplish in the face of rugged nature if he is left in peace. There in the valley of the rapid Derwent, with the moors and mountains of the Peak sullenly towering away to the West and North, there protected by hanging woods and friendly hills, soothed by innumerable waterfalls and streams, made beautiful with a tapestry of green pastures, serenely rise the great wings and terraces of Chatsworth, the statue of Pallas Athene on the point of the west pediment proudly surveying that wonderful landscape, and challenging nature with the art and the wisdom of men.

It was intolerable that all this beauty and well-being

21

should be exposed, as the Duke of Newcastle had said in his letter, to the insults and attacks of a "lawless and rebellious multitude." Perhaps, as the Duke of Devonshire looked at the numberless frescoes of classical themes painted by Verrio and Laguerre and Thornhill which adorned the ante-chambers, the staircases and the state apartments at Chatsworth, his eye lighted with expectancy on the scenes commemorating the fall of Phæthon. This insolent young man, Prince Charles Edward, might conquer Scotland in the course of a few weeks and hold his Court in the Palace of Holyrood: in nine months' time he would be less than the dust, a hunted fugitive in the heather!

Meanwhile the Duke had to cope with the crisis as it affected his county. The Privy Council, meeting at Kensington Palace on September 5th, 1745, had decided to put into execution the laws, some of them dating back to Elizabeth's reign, against "Papists, reputed Papists and Non-Jurors, being dangerous to His Majesty's Government": such persons *inter alia* must take the oaths and subscribe declarations, and if they failed to do so should not be allowed to retain any fire-arms, etc. (other than necessary weapons allowed by order of the Justices for self-defence), or horses of any value, and Popish Recusants must repair to their places of abode and not remove five miles therefrom without licence. " And so," ended the Privy Council's letter to the Duke, "we bid Your Grace very heartily, Farewell." The Duke immediately forwarded this letter to the Clerk of the Peace at Derby, one Mr. Joseph Hayne, with this laconic message: "The enclosed Letter of

Council came to me by last night's Post, which I desire you to lay before the Justices of the Peace in the usual manner." That was the Duke's way with business letters—the shorter the better. Later on—early in November—when Mr. Hayne broke into a dithyramb about the Duke and his ancestors, their patriotism, the Constitution—

"in great measure obtained for us by the wise Councills and Activities of your Noble Grandfather (the great Patriot of his Country) in the Eminent share He had in procuring the happy Revolution at a Crisis when destruction was at hand"—

praying for blessings to be "enjoyed by all Ages of Your Illustrious Family whilst this Orb exists," and so on, the Duke merely replied with:

"thanks for the pacquet I rec'd last night, and shall be much obliged if you will take the trouble to state the acc'ts of the several Companies" [of the Duke's volunteer regiment just raised].[1]

There are a number of letters among the Chatsworth manuscripts showing how the Roman Catholics were feared and suspected—unjustly as it turned out—at this time. Thus, Thomas Gisborne, a notable magistrate of Derby, writes to the Duke on September 14th, reporting that the Justices have tendered the oaths, "to some Little Rascalls

[1] Robert Simpson's *Collection of Fragments Illustrative of the History of Derby*, 2 vols., 1826, contains the Privy Council letter and Hayne correspondence, and I am indebted to it for filling in gaps in the Chatsworth MSS.

amongst us who all took 'em," while one John Griffith, writing on September 25th, expresses himself as apprehensive of "ye R.C.: and our Disaffected neighbours even more so than from the Rebells at present." If there should be an invasion, "your Grace may depend upon it they will then Rise, for different Parts, and that they have a Watch-word for ye purpose." The same correspondent, writing from Wentworth House in Yorkshire on September 30th, reports that the Archbishop of York and others "apprehend something Deeply laid and Dark from ye R.C. and that Speedy Care ought to be taken of them."

Then there was a mysterious paper forwarded by Lord Malton. This document runs as follows:

"There are two persons in the Parish of Hathersage that are able to depose if compelled to it, their sight of a great number of arms concealed in two private rooms at the Duke of Norfolk's, whose names are Robert Ashton and Ann Ashton. They saw the same at Worksop Manner. Be cautious in the search; For the within mention'd Rooms have no passage into them, but from the Top of the Leads; the taking up of some part of which will discover the passage into them."

The Duke of Newcastle asks the Duke of Devonshire— "as the persons therein mentioned live pretty near Chatsworth"—to have affidavits taken, and generally to be active in having the matter quickly investigated.

Perhaps the most amusing letter is one from a Mr. H. Johnston, who writes to the Duke of Devonshire from Stoke-Ash in the county of Suffolk. Mr. Johnston says he has been "a fortnight in the country from which your Grace takes the name of Cavendish" and from an acquaintance of some twenty-two years knows all there is to know about people within a radius of twenty or thirty miles from Stoke-Ash. He thinks what he says may be helpful to the Ministry in "this Critical Juncture." The people have been corrupted by "the Romish Clergy or rather the Romish families at several distances—the seminaries of which were transplanted from the Nurserys of Lord Petre in Essex"; moreover the promotion of "ignorant and sycophantical young men" in Church of England orders has also done damage. Mr. Johnston then proceeds:

"The spirit of the people . . . will be animated by the Roast Beef of Old England and keeping them rather better than they live themselves wch. is exceeding well. And as his Majesty has been graciously some time since pleased to pardon a great [number] of Smugglers I am of opinion that 200 of those men, put them under a Decemvir and under the command of two Centurions or the matter may be adjusted by military wisdom, would be of greater service than all the Militia of the County—provided any Invasion should happen in any of the Maritime parts of the County."

Mr. Johnston ends by subscribing himself "with the greatest truth," etc.

Sir Thomas Abney, a Derbyshire neighbour of the Duke's, had more than once written expressing his apprehensions of disaffection in many English counties, and suggesting that the Justices of the Peace should meet at Derby, though he feared the attendance would be poor unless His Grace is pleased "to lead us." But this His Grace had every intention of doing. Other Dukes, notably of Bedford, Richmond, Montagu and Rutland were raising regiments. These would serve anywhere in Great Britain and be paid from the Exchequer, whereas provincial regiments would serve only in their county and would be financed by local effort. In both cases arms would be supplied by the Government. The distinction between the two kinds of regiment, as just described, is summed up in a letter from the Prime Minister to the Duke of Devonshire dated from Arlington Street on October 5th. In the same letter Pelham refers to the fine spirit being displayed in Yorkshire, where "the Archbishop has immortalised himself by his behaviour." This was Thomas Herring, Archbishop of York, and later of Canterbury, through whose efforts and those of Lord Malton very large sums were subscribed and troops of horse and infantry raised in Yorkshire.

"Even the Tories," Pelham observed, "do well on this occasion," inspired, it appears, by the Archbishop's leadership. The Archbishop took a very serious view of the situation, as is clear from an illuminating letter to Philip Yorke dated November 9th, from Bishopsthorpe, published in Yorke's *Hardwicke*: "for their horses' hoofs are of flint and their wheels like a whirlwind," he wrote of the rebels, and added, "for my own part, I am far from thinking that victory with us is infallible, but you may imagine I don't propagate this doctrine."

On Saturday, September 28th, at 12 o'clock, at the George

26

Inn in Derby, the Duke of Devonshire presided over a great meeting of the " Gentlemen and Clergy of the County." We learn from the contemporary *Derby Mercury* (quoted in Simpson's *Collection*) that

"a grand entertainment was provided for them at the aforesaid Inn, the expense of which was generously defrayed by his Grace. After dinner a subscription was begun, and signed by the Gentlemen present,"

who had already "cheerfully" entered into and signed an association as follows:

"Whereas, a most wicked and unnatural Rebellion is begun in that part of Great Britain called Scotland, by the eldest son of the Pretender, against our rightful sovereign King George, in order to subvert our Religion and Liberties, and to entail Popery and Slavery on us and our Posterity: We his Majesty's most Loyal Subjects, whose names are hereunto subscribed, do hereby declare our utmost abhorrence of so wicked an attempt; and in the most solemn manner engage, that we will, at the hazard of our Lives and Fortunes, Support and defend our excellent Constitution in Church and State, and oppose all attempts against his Majesty's Person and Government, particularly the Rebellion now carried on in favour of a Popish abjured Pretender. And we hereby promise and engage to meet together from time to time to concert and execute such measures as may be necessary for effecting the purposes of this our Association."

The association was signed by the Duke, Lord Hartington, Sir Nathaniel Curzon and a great number of well-known

Derbyshire names—Meynell, Fitzherbert, Okeover, Pole, Harpur, Vernon, Wilmot, Port and so on.[1]

Then, on October 3rd, at the King's Head, another meeting was held, when it was agreed to raise six hundred men formed into two companies, "of which the Marquis of Hartington and Sir Nathaniel Curzon, Bart., the two knights of the Shire, in Parliament, were appointed Colonels." The meeting at the King's Head was followed on Friday, October 28th, by one at the Talbot—indeed the Derby inns must have done well out of the Rebellion—when further steps were taken towards the mobilisation of the regiment. Captains were to be paid 8s. a day, corporals 1s. 3d., drummer ditto, "private men" 1s. For "Bounty money at 5s. a piece, and for Trophys, by which are meant Halbards, Drums, and other little necessarys," £20 was allotted to each of twelve companies of 58 officers and men. The men when enlisted were to be quartered by each captain of a company "at such publick houses in your neighbourhood as is most convenient to you." As to uniforms, the hatters and clothiers of Derby were set vigorously to work.

It appears from a document printed in Simpson's

[1] The name of my ancestor (grandfather to the third great) John Beresford, a country squire of Ashbourne and Bentley (1687–1755), is conspicuous by its absence. I had long suspected that he was a Jacobite (as his father, also John Beresford, Esq., D.L., certainly was): for instance, he made his will on January 30th, 1754, January 30th being the anniversary of the execution of Charles I. But my suspicion is now confirmed by the fact that he offered hospitality in 1741 to a non-juring parson —the Rev. Thos. Bedford, as is pointed out by Mr. Eardley Simpson in his *Derby and the Forty-Five*, p. 33.

Collection of Fragments Illustrating the History and Antiquities of Derby that subscription for the purpose of the association and regiment was by no means universal. "On Monday last," High Constable Robotham reports, "I was at Pleasley, but all the Freeholders wholely but the parson which is expected to subscribe, were gone to Lenton fair." Then follows a list of persons who refused to subscribe. Others said "they would consider of it," and others again were "not at home."

It is significant of the anxiety and uncertainty felt by the Government as to the degree of Jacobite feeling in a number of counties that the Militia—the normal means of domestic defence—was not called out, and it was evidently the opinion of the Duke of Devonshire that it would be unwise to raise the Militia in Derbyshire. "Mr. Pelham and I," wrote Lord Herbert to the Duke on September 21st, "concur with your Grace in your Sentiments concerning the difficulties at this time attending the raising of the Militia, for which reason he gives the preference, as you see, to Associations." There were not lacking those who feared treachery, and one Joseph Offley writes to the Duke of Devonshire on September 22nd, saying: "there is a report that a neighbour I mention'd has arms for 1500 men."

On the same day—September 28th—that the Duke of Devonshire was holding his great meeting of Derbyshire gentlemen and clergy at the George Inn, the Prime Minister wrote to him with news from the centre of things. The Duke of Cumberland, commanding the army in Flanders, had been ordered to send back more battalions, "which are to land at Newcastle in case that place continues in our hands"—the doubt is typical of Pelham's pessimistic mind; Pelham fears that Edinburgh Castle will fall; Marshal Wade with 10,000 men has been ordered to Doncaster; eight squadrons of dragoons have been sent for from Flanders:

"it is the opinion of all our Generals not to divide our little Army, for if we did, we shall probably be beat in detail . . . the fatal experience we have had from the defeat of Cope, I hope will satisfy all friends that the Government act rightly."

The Prime Minister with melancholy prescience—though his words just then must have been a little damping to the Duke of Devonshire—concludes:

"I doubt your provincial guard, if the Rebels come your way, will not be a sufficient security; I hope you will not think so, and take care of yourself and family in time! But if our accounts are true, you are in no danger, the Rebels being, it is said, determined to keep possession of Scotland."

On Monday, October 7th, 1745, Pelham writes:

"I am afraid it will be a great while before Wade gets Northward, he is set out but his army marches but slowly. My House is full, I scarce know what I write, but was unwilling your servant should go back without an answer.
I am my dear Duke,
Ever yours,
H. PELHAM."

Four days later the Duke of Newcastle sent an exceedingly

to be most probable that the Duke of Devonshire himself
repaired to London to be present at the opening of Parliament by George II on October 17th, though it is clear that
he must have returned immediately after the ceremony.
Secondly, Lord Hartington was in London for the opening
of Parliament, and for the rest of the month, and kept his
father perfectly in touch with events.

On October 20th Lord Hartington wrote to his father
conveying news from the Pelham brothers; in particular
the Duke of Newcastle

"desired me to tell you that the Letters from abroad are
not very agreable, the Dutch are in a great hurry to make
a peace and want to include us in it and desire that we will
consent to restore Cape Breton immediately."

As the capture of Cape Breton from the French by the
combined efforts of the British Navy and the New England
Colonists in June of this year had been the one decisive
success of the war, the Dutch suggestion was singularly
unpalatable to Englishmen. Hartington continues:

"All the Ministry have received Letters that the Papists
intend to rise as tomorrow, but no credit is given to it but
I believe some care will be taken to have a stronger Guard
than usual. I hope you got safe to Chatsworth.
                    I am
                 Dr. Sr.
                    Your most dutifull Son
                                HARTINGTON.
I beg my Duty to
my Mother."

On October 26th Lord Hartington, who had been actively seeing about arms for the Duke's volunteer regiment, writes:

"The arms will set out from the Tower on Monday morning, the Steward has been so ill of the Gout that it was impossible for him to take any care about them: I was forced to trouble Sir Robt. Willmot . . . there has been some difficulty about his indenting for them."

Hearing rumours that the rebels were on the point of invading England, Lord Hartington had been immediately to see Mr. Pelham:

"but he was just gone to Esher; I went to Court and found the Duke of Newcastle, and told him that as I heard the Rebells were coming our way I could not possibly think of staying here, he said that he thought at present it was very uncertain and that it would be wrong for me to go before the King was acquainted with it, and that if he had any intelligence he would certainly let me know it, and if they came on would speak to the King on Monday morning; you will certainly know if they are coming, and in that case I should be much oblig'd to you if you would send the Black Mare to Derby, because you may depend upon it that I will at all events set out upon the first news. . . . I have directed the Arms to Mr. Gisborne at Derby. I wish the Drums etc. may be ready to be sent down with them.

Yr. most dutifull son
HARTINGTON."

Three days later, on Saturday, October 29th, he writes again:

34

"The Arms were loaded on two Wagons at the Tower yesterday, but I believe did not leave London till this morning (Saturday) and will be at Derby on Monday next. There are 28 Chests containing 700 Musquets, 700 Bayonets, 300 and 90 Cartouch Boxes and 900 and 50 Frogs which are things to carry the Bayonets in, the remaining number of the two last Articles will be sent down as soon as they can be made, for they had no more ready at the Tower. . . . Mr. Pelham had a Letter from Wade dated the 26, who does not seem to think that the Rebells will come forward. . . ." **1434423**

There are three more letters from Lord Hartington to the Duke of Devonshire, dated October 31st, November 2nd, and November 5th, of which the following are extracts:

Oct. 31st, 1745. ". . . The Rebels . . . are said to be in great confusion. . . . I hope by the next post to be able to send you word when I shall come down, I should hope to set out about the middle of next week. The Tories, I hear, are going out of Town; if so there will be no occasion for my stay. . . . The Steward is so ill that he is not able to write to my Mother but he will take care to obey her orders; and a Hogshead of Madeira will set out on Monday. . . ."

Nov. 2nd, 1745. ". . . I think to set out some time next week, scarce before Thursday. . . . I had almost forgot to tell you that Lord Barrington complimented you in the House of Lords for what you had done in Derbyshire. . . ."

Nov. 5th, 1745. Political gossip chiefly; talk of an invasion from Dunkirk. ". . . The Scotch and Irish Regiments in the French Service are all ordered down there. . . ."

Lord Hartington's letters show that the Prime Minister opened his mind freely to him, especially about foreign affairs, and they reveal the anxiety caused by Pitt's uncertain tactics in semi-opposition. In one of the letters there is a reference to the Duke of Grafton, who was Lord Chamberlain—it should be remembered that the great officers of the King's household were members of the Cabinet at this period[1]—going down to Euston for fox-hunting despite the crisis of invasion and foreign affairs. Lord Anson dines with Hartington one day and confirms the loss of a man-of-war commanded by Captain Saumarez, which had been chasing French ships.

It is significant of the length of time which it took for news of affairs in Scotland to reach London that Lord Hartington was ignorant, when writing on November 5th, that Prince Charles Edward's army was already on the move. The Prince's forces had concentrated at Dalkeith on October 31st, and thereafter started on their march into England in two columns, the one commanded by the Prince himself and Lord George Murray advancing via Kelso in the direction of Newcastle, the other under the Jacobite Dukes of Athol and Perth by Moffat in the direction of Carlisle, but the Prince's march to Kelso and along the Northumberland border was to deceive Marshal Wade into thinking that Newcastle—where the British troops were stationed—was the object of attack. We know from the Chevalier Johnstone's admirable memoirs that the

[1] See, for instance, the list of the Cabinet Council appended to Lord Hervey's *Memoirs*, Vol. III, pp. 358-9.

march was so well planned and the secret of ultimate destination so well kept in the invading army itself that "we were very much surprised on finding ourselves all arrive, on 9th November, almost at the same instant, on a heath in England, about a quarter of a league from the town of Carlisle." The total force under Prince Charles Edward did not much exceed 5,000, of which some 500 were cavalry, but as the main part of the army consisted of Highlanders and consequently—as the Duke of Devonshire had observed—"devilish good marchers," their mobility was far beyond that of the British troops. These, to resist the invasion, consisted of Marshal Wade's army at Newcastle—some 10,000 horse and foot, while another force under the command of Sir John Ligonier was now being concentrated to advance from the south into the midland and northern counties, as required. This force, of which the Duke of Cumberland—who had been summoned over from Flanders—ultimately took command on November 27th at Lichfield, amounted to perhaps 8,000 or 10,000 horse and foot. Early in December an effort was made to collect together some further troops on Finchley Common. The superior weight of numbers of the British troops is frequently emphasised, and therefore the forlorn character of the Prince's project. It is too often forgotten that the Prince had three powerful allies—first, superior mobility; secondly, the Government's uncertainty (until the rebels had reached Derby) whether the English Jacobites would rise; and thirdly, the Government's constant apprehensions that the French preparations both at Brest and Dunkirk would mature into a formidable invasion. The unfortunate friction between the King and his principal Ministers, and the incompetence or sinister inactivity of one of them—Lord Tweeddale, the Secretary for Scotland, who was in close association with Lord Granville—were factors favourable to the invaders. We know from the correspondence published by Coxe in his *Pelham Administration* how critical was the situation when the news of Preston Pans reached London, the Duke of Newcastle avowing that, had not the reinforcements from Flanders arrived the day before the news of Sir John Cope's defeat came,

"the confusion to the City of London would not have been to be described, and the King's crown, I will venture to say, in the utmost danger."

It is clear from the Chatsworth correspondence, which is here published for the first time,[1] that throughout these months the responsible heads of the Government took the most serious, and in the case of the Prime Minister, a pessimistic view of the situation.

Almost immediately after his last letter of November 5th Lord Hartington must have set out from London and posted or coached to Derby, riding from the latter place to Chatsworth on his black mare. For, on November 9th, Henry Pelham writes to him that there are very contradictory messages about the movements of the rebels towards

[1] Mr. Eardley Simpson's recent *Derby and the Forty-Five* contains some quotations from the Chatsworth MSS., but they do not exceed some 350 words in all.

England: meanwhile Wade is waiting at Newcastle and General Sir John Ligonier is preparing to move his troops as soon as possible. There are reports from Scotland of embarkations from Dunkirk:

"it is said also that the D. of Ormond or Ld. Marshal are coming over with 10,000 men, this may be said to keep up the spirits of the Jacobites."

On November 15th the Duke of Newcastle wrote as follows from Whitehall to the Duke of Devonshire:

MY LORD,

His Majesty having received certain Advice that the Rebels, and the Pretender's Son with them, have march'd into Cumberland, and, according to all Appearances intend to advance Southward; tho' it is as yet uncertain what route they will take: His Majesty has commanded me to recommend it in a particular manner to your Grace, in case the Rebels should attempt to come into the County of Derby, to take the most effectual measures for obstructing their passage, and distressing them by all possible Means, and particularly by rendering it as difficult, as maybe, for them to procure Subsistence and Forage; and that your Grace will also take the best care you can, that the King's Troops may be supplied with Subsistence and Forage. And your Grace will be pleased to give the proper Directions, that a number of Deputy Lieutenants and Justices of the Peace should frequently meet at certain proper Places, to be appointed, for that Purpose, as long as the Rebels shall remain in the Neighbourhood.

I am etc.,
HOLLES NEWCASTLE.

On the same day that the Duke of Newcastle wrote this letter Carlisle surrendered to the Prince, and shortly afterwards the rebel army set out on its further march southward. Expresses sent to the Duke of Devonshire from Penrith on November 19th apprised him that:

"the Highland Army is swarming in here all this day like bees. Those we had last night are all gone the Lancashire Road. . . . The whole body is undoubtedly moving this way. Their's are all forced Marches. Numbers never stop."

The Duke of Devonshire, on receipt of the Duke of Newcastle's letter, and of these expresses, made immediate arrangements to confer with the Justices and Deputy Lieutenants of Derbyshire, on Monday, November 25th, at Ashbourne. The Duke suggested the post office as the rendezvous, but, being apprised by the Clerk of the Peace that the post office in Ashbourne was a private house and the postmaster a tradesman, the meeting was arranged at the Black Moor's Head. This was doubtless also more convenient for the essential dinner which was ordered "for 1 o'clock exactly."[1]

Probably it was at this meeting that a decision was reached to cut the roads at Buxton and elsewhere so as to embarrass the march of the rebels, for there is a solicitous letter from Alexander Barker, the Duke's steward, written at 5 a.m. on Saturday, November 30th, asking:

[1] See Robert Simpson's *Collection of Fragments Illustrative of the History of Derby*, 2 vols., 1826, pp. 212–63, to which reference has already been made (footnote, p. 23).

"if there should be any trees by the Road does yr. Grace
please to have them thrown cross it, or if any Hollows
should they be filled in: I shall give directions only for
three Cutts without I hear from your Grace; . . . if there
be time a cut or two might be made over the Turnpike
between Whaley and Chappell but shall not do that without
yr. Grace's further directions."

The Duke and Lord Hartington were now at Derby, at
the George Inn, whither they had ridden from Chatsworth
on November 29th, summoning the captains and companies
of the volunteer regiment. It was already known in Derby
that the rebels were approaching Manchester—they reached
Manchester that day, and on December 1st marched on to
Macclesfield. Meanwhile Marshal Wade had made an
entirely ineffectual march westward from Newcastle with
a view to relieving Carlisle. But when he reached Hexham
he heard that Carlisle had fallen. The country was deep in
snow—it was an appalling winter, setting in early—and he
returned to Newcastle on November 22nd.

Lord Hartington, writing to his friend Dr. Newcombe
on November 18th from Chatsworth, refers to Wade's
march westward before its abortive result was known, and
when Hartington himself was still hopeful that the rebels
would not advance beyond Carlisle:

DEAR SR.

I intended fully to have wrote to you from London, but
the news of the Rebels coming to England, prevented me
by putting me into some hurry as it obliged me to leave

41

London sooner than I intended; the last accounts we had
from the North was that the Rebels entered Carlisle on
Friday; it is said the Castle may hold out eight days but
I very much doubt it. Mr. Wade marched from Newcastle
Saturday and was to be at Carlisle Tuesday but the badness
of the weather will I am afraid make him longer. My own
opinion is that the Rebels will not come forward, for if
that had been their scheme, they would never have lost so
much time at Carlisle. It was with great difficulty that the
Highlanders were prevailed upon to march into England,
and I have a great notion that they will retire back before
Mr. Wade gets up to them. We have laid expresses from
hence to Manchester by which we have very early intel-
ligences; the next accounts which we expect every minute
will clear up all doubts, for if they intend to come forwards
they will most certainly have begun their march; we are all
in very good spirits, our companies are raised, well arm'd
and ready to march if there is occasion, and I hope we shall
all behave very well. The men are very willing to go. People
of all sorts have behaved very well. The County have raised
six hundred men which they maintain at their own expence
without any assistance from the Government, having neither
pay nor rank. But I am strongly persuaded that we shall
have no occasion to show our courage, for Mr. Wade will
certainly do the Business for us; it is, to be sure, very right
to be prepared for the worst, but I thank God I am not of
a desponding Nature; if any accident should happen to
Mr. Wade, we must then all go, and no one will go more
cheerfully and willingly than I shall, as I think it indis-
pensably my Duty. If our affairs are well over I hope to
meet you in London soon after Christmas, but it will be
some time before I shall leave this country. I beg my

compliments to Mrs. Newcombe, the Duke, and to Dr.
Cheyney.
I am,
Dr. Sir,
Yours most sincerely,
HARTINGTON.

"Thank God I am not of a desponding Nature"! Well!
that could hardly be said of others, certainly not of the
Prime Minister, who suffered from recurrent waves of
depression despite his great abilities and the very substantial
services rendered to the country during his Ministry. Even
Henry Fox,[1] writing from London to Lord Hartington on
November 19th, referring anxiously to Wade's march
towards the rebels, and expressing "a strong opinion that
the event will be in our Favour" cannot forbear to observe:
"yet surely one is too often put in mind of poor Ld.
Orford's [Sir Robert Walpole's] prophecy: 'This Crown
will be fought for *aequo Marte.*' I daresay yr. Lordship has
heard him say so." Fox concludes his letter with that
courtesy, formal and yet affectionate, which is one of the
charms of eighteenth-century correspondence:

"Give me leave to beg my best and most sincere Compliments to the Duke of Devonshire, and to assure your Lordship that you have not in the world a more affectionate and
faithfull Humble Servant than your most oblig'd and most
Obedt.
H. FOX."

On November 19th the Prime Minister wrote to the

[1] Afterwards the first Lord Holland, at this time Surveyor-General of
Works and a Lord of the Treasury.

Duke of Devonshire one of his characteristic letters, un-
varnished and at the same time vivid, disillusioned but
warm-hearted, giving an account of the situation in London.
After explaining that he fears that the army of Ligonier—
General Sir John Ligonier, whose name he spells Legonier
and, for short, "Leg"—won't be able to rendezvous at
Warrington till the first week in December, he continues:

"And I am sorry to tell you that I think his state of
health is so bad, that without an extraordinary and sudden
alteration, it will be impossible for him to go thro' this
affair. I dined with him this day at Newcastle House,
where I found him so altered that I should scarce think him
the same man; he is sensible of it himself, and has desired
that General Hawley be sent for over, to take the command
in case he should not be able to go through with it; it will
be some time before he can get there, till then Anstruther
and the Duke of Richmond are the two first Officers. I
mention these things to you, but it would be better not to
tell of 'em, till we see how Leg. goes on. Our accounts say
the town of Carlisle has capitulated, bringing £2,000 to the
Rebels. The Castle, they say, is determined to hold out,
and it is hoped will be able to do so till Wade comes to their
relief. I don't hear that [Wade's] army is in the best condi-
tion, nor that all the Officers have an equal dependance one on
the other; I dare say the Old Man [Wade was now seventy-
two] will act for the best, and if he can come to a fair field of
Battle I should not despair of success. We must hope for the
best, I pray God this may soon be decided, for if it is not, all
our accounts from abroad open a sad scene. It is pretty
certain that France will support the Pretender openly, and I
hear from good hands that the Duke of Richlieu and most

of their favourite Officers are destined for this service. Amidst these general misfortunes, I cannot help mentioning our particular situations att home. The K—g frightened yet impracticable, some of our new Allys [the group of politicians, of whom Pitt was the outstanding figure, who were anxious to be taken into the Ministry and, until they had succeeded in their object, were uncommonly embarassing friends] fill'd with most extraordinary notions, and even now stipulating what we shall or shall not do with regard to foreign Affairs, before the rebellion is put to an end. Your cousin Bedford and his father-in-law talk and act reasonably, but the House of Commons people are most extravagant and unreasonable. What all this will end in, God only knows. But it makes me wish you here; you know best whether it is proper or convenient for you to come away, but some resolution must soon be taken; I should be sorry to determine without your Grace's approbation. Your brother Roper keeps in Suffolk following his pleasures out of harm's way, I wish the rest of your friends were in the same happy state. The rest of the Brittish Cavalry are sent for, and I believe the Hessians will follow them soon, but that is not yet absolutely determined. My services to Hartington and all friends at Chatsworth. I am glad Lord Granby has been with you, the Duke of Rutland is much changed since he has commenced soldier. I hope a good use may be made of this incident. Cat:[?Carteret] talks more reasonably, and I believe is frightened for his *Money*.

    I am My dear Lord Duke

      Your Grace's most obedient and most humble Servt.

                    H. Pelham.''

On December 3rd, the day before the rebel army entered Derby, the Prime Minister wrote a pleasant, gossipy letter to

Lord Hartington, actually cracking a joke or two—little aware of the bewildering excursions and alarums through which his friends were passing at that moment. Before relating these we open Henry Pelham's letter and read as follows:

My dear Lord

I most heartily thank you upon your kind congratulations on the Birth of a young Linky [he is referring to the birth of his grandson George Clinton born on November 26th, the first son of his daughter Catherine and Henry, Earl of Lincoln]; the Father is as happy as the Grandfather, and I hope, before it is very long, to return you my compliments on the same fortunate event [the Prime Minister is being rather skittish, as Lady Charlotte Boyle, Lord Hartington's fiancée, was only just fourteen: however he was able to congratulate them almost exactly three years later]. Your friends in Picadilly [the Burlingtons] are come to town, I have not seen them, but hear they are well. We have been alarmed lately on the supposed march of the Rebels your way, but, by an express which came from Lord Lonsdale this day, it seems out of doubt that they intend for Wales. He says they all left Manchester last Monday, that one part of their force went the Stockport road, the others the Knutsford, but that it was supposed they would all meet in the latter. If so the Duke [i.e. the Duke of Cumberland, always referred to simply as *the Duke*] will probably come to a Battel with 'em, and tho I see 'em a set of desperate men, yet I can't but think a superiority of regular troops, which the Duke certainly has with him, must beat 'em out of the field. We have also rumours of gatherings in Scotland, and some Foreign Troops being landed; how true this is I can't say, for I have not seen a letter to the Government from thence, since you

left us: a fine way for Ministers to support a Prince, when one part of the Administration does not acquaint the other with what passes, even in a Rebellion [this is a shaft at the incompetent Lord Tweeddale, Secretary of State for Scotland, and illustrates the absence of Cabinet unity in the eighteenth century]. I wrote to the Duke of Devonshire, and sent my letter to Litchfield, where I heard he was, but since he was not there I should be glad to hear whether he received my letter or not. The Duke seems much pleased with your father's engaging to break up the roads in Derbyshire; if the times did not require more seriousness, I would crack a joke with you upon endeavouring to make Derbyshire roads more uneven than they naturally are. There is a letter just now come in from a man employ'd by the Government, which says the Rebels were to be last night at Macclesfield; that the Duke's army was within 12 miles of 'em, which, if true, must produce a battel this day or tomorrow. Pray God grant us good success. I am not afraid, yet cannot but be extremely anxious as to the success. You will hear it soon, it cannot be long before we shall; if things end well I am of opinion foreign invasions will cease when private and domestic quiet arises. Amongst the many blessings will attend a thorough defeat of the rebels, that of seeing you oftener, and enjoying ourselves the rest of our days in more quiet than we have done of late will with me not be one of the least. I hope in God you will have no more apprehensions of a visit your way, and of consequence that attendance which you now properly pay to your country will have its end.
I am
My Dear Lord Hartington
Most affectionately and faithfully yrs.
H. PELHAM.

47

It was during these early days of December that the rebel army carried out those brilliant manœuvres which constitute the crisis of the invasion. They had reached Macclesfield on their southward march on December 1st. The Duke of Cumberland, who had now taken over the command of the central army from Sir John Ligonier, had concentrated his forces first at Coventry and Lichfield and subsequently at Stone, with the vanguard at Newcastle-under-Lyme. The concentration at Stone had taken place because Lord George Murray with part of the rebel army had made a feint in the direction of Congleton, and Cumberland thought—as Pelham had thought—that the objective was Wales. The road to Derby through Leek and Ashbourne was now open: Lord George Murray advanced rapidly through these places, followed a little later by Prince Charles Edward, and on December 4th the two columns successively entered Derby in triumph. Cumberland, in a fever of anxiety lest the rebels should hasten on towards London, rushed his troops back by forced marches to Stafford, Lichfield, and Coventry, intending to intercept the rebels at Northampton. As a consequence of all this rapid marching forwards and backwards the royal army was thoroughly exhausted, without food, with worn-out shoes and clothes in rags. There was little straw, and cover at night was hard to find in the wintry nights.[1]

Among the Chatsworth papers there is a brief letter to the Duke of Devonshire written in the clear, firm hand of the

[1] See Sir Evan Charteris's *Duke of Cumberland*, ch. xviii, and the vivid correspondence in Yorke's *Hardwicke*, ch. xiv.

Duke of Cumberland, which gives a vivid idea of the situation of his army when he first heard that the rebels had out-manœuvred him. The letter is sealed with Cumberland's royal seal and is endorsed simply on the back:

The Duke 3 Dec. 1745

To the Duke of Devonshire
Stone, Dec. ye. 3 1745

MY LORD after the most fatiguing 24 hours for troops that can be imagined we are forced to retire back to Stafford and from thence I believe for Darbyshire. This is all occasioned by a counter-march of the rebells to Leake & and this night for Cheadle so that I fear they may be able to get there before me. No pains or trouble shall be spared but the weather is such that should we not have a halt this night the troops would be quite jaded.

I send this by your own servant for expedition that you may be aprised of their coming: this moment a man is come in who heard ask for a guide to Ashbourn. I am your affectionate friend

WILLIAM.

P.S. Should we come your way I hope that we shall find meat and bread for the soldiers.

On the day when this letter was written the Duke of Devonshire was in Derby with his regiment of 600 volunteers and 120 men raised by himself and " kept at his own expense." It was plainly futile for this small half-trained force of some 700 men to attempt to withstand the onset of 5,000 Highlanders who had proved themselves more than a match for the King's regular army, not only on the battle-field but in tactical march and manœuvre. The account of the rapid retreat of the volunteer force to Nottingham will be related hereafter in the frank account of Lord Hartington. Meanwhile, through the eyes of William Bateman, Town Clerk of Derby, we will take a very realistic and critical view of the rebel host quartered in Derby. The first part of this account was published by Mr. Bateman, as he himself says, in the *Derby Mercury* of his day and the *Gentleman's Magazine* of 1746. The latter part has never been published before. As the whole account is extremely vivid and amusing I give it in full from a manuscript among the Chatsworth papers.

"A true Relation of the Behaviour, as well as the Description, of such part of the Rebells which were quartered at the House of Wm. Bateman Town Clerk in Derby, during their continuance there.

Be it Remember'd that on Wednesday the 4th day of Decem^r. 1745 The Rebels marched from Ashbourne to Derby with their pretended prince and his Adherents, the first Division or Vanguard of Horse came here abt. 12 o'clock in the morning, and others continued coming in till about 8 at night with their Artillery; [they] were supposed to be about 6, or 7000^d, tho they gave out they were 9000^d or more. they stayed till ffriday Morning.

The delightful Complim^t. of them quarter'd on me by Billet, about six o'clock on Wednesday Evening, were 6 Officers (one a Major as they stiled him) 40 private Men, with 8 picked up Shabby Horses, some with^t. Saddles or Bridles, others with Halters, and pieces of Bridles and Ropes about their Heads and Necks, and poor Saddles or a Sort of Padds stuffed with Straw upon them.

Most of these Men after their entrance into my House

(I tho^t) looked like so many ffiends just turned out of Hell,
to ravage the Kingdom, and cut throats, and under their
Plaids, nothing but a various sort of Butchering weapons,
were to be seen; the Sight at first must be thought (as it
really was) very Shocking and horrible; But these Wretches
being fatigued with their long March from Leek on Wednesday, soon after they came into my House, stuffed themselves well with Bread Cheese and Ale, and then about 20 of
'em before a great ffire in my Hall, order'd by them, call'd
for a large quantity of Straw and nestled into it for Repose,
and the Remaind^r of them did the like in a large Laundry
Room belonging to my House before two great ffires
likewise order'd to be made there. The Officers took
possession of my Parlour and Chambers they liked best,
commanded what Supper and Liquor they would have, and
expected me (tho in great pain with the Gout) my Wife and
whole ffamily, to wait on them as if they were born so many
petty princes, yet one of the Officers was tolerably civil and
communicative, and really redressed some complaints made
about the ill behaviour of his Men; My Hall after these
Vagabond Creatures began to be warm, by such Numbers
under the Straw, and a great ffire near them, Stunk so of
their itch and other nastinesses about them, as if they had
been so many persons in a condemned Hole, and 'twill be
very happy if they've left no contagion, behind them. The
next day (Thursday) the Officers and their Men grew more
bold and insolent, order'd in an haughty tone, what Meat
and Drink they would have at their Meals, and if you was
not at an instant ready to administer what they called for,
some of them would surround you with fierce and savage
Looks, as if they had been (in my comparison) so many Mutes
appointed to Strangle or some other way Assassin you. In

this short time they eat me up near a side of Beef, 8 joints of Mutton, 4 Cheeses with abundance of white and brown Bread, particularly white, 3 couple of ffowls, and would have Drams continually as well as strong Beer Ale Tea etc. But really what did afford me some matter for an unavoidable Laughter (tho my Family in this miserable Situation) was to see these Desperadoes, from Officers to their common Men, at their several Meals, first pull off their Bonnetts, and then lift up their eyes in a most solemn manner, and mutter something to themselves by way of saying Grace, as if they had been born so many pure primitive Christians. As to their Dialect or Language, (from the idea I had of it) the same seem'd to be as if an Hord of Hottentots, wild Monkys in a Desert, or Vagrant Gypsies, had been jabbering, screaming, and howling together, and really this jargon of Speech was very properly suited to such a Sett of Banditti. I can't omit taking notice of another singular circumstance relating to these Gentry, and that is of the generous present they made me at Parting on Friday morning for the trouble and expense I was at, and the dangers undergone (tho by the by I wished for no other compensation than the escape of my Family with their lives and of my House being plunder'd) which was a Regiment or two of Highland Lice, several Loads of their filthy Excrement, and other Ejections of different colours, scattered before my Door, in the Garden, and elsewhere about my House, in the sight of all the Family, together with their wishes for a speedy Meeting again at Derby with their prince crown'd with victory and peace. A true Portrait of those who would be our Rulers! But may God avert such an Event and grant that the English protestants (from the specimen so lately exhibited of the principles and schemes of these moroding and wandering Thieves) may soon hear of their utter extirpation. Anti-Pretender and Highlander. (Dulce est pro patria Mori)——

N.B. The religion of some of these common creatures (if they had any at all) seem'd to be a medley of Heathenism and popery, with a little tincture of the Scotch Kirk, but after all this complication of odd matter there did not appear the least Stricture of Humanity amongst them. So far I put in the Derby paper, wch. after got into the Magazine and other Publick prints."

He continues:

"In respect of the Treatment I recd. myself from others of these Miscreants not quarter'd at my House 'twas in this manner. That when they had been a little settled in their Quarters on Wednesday Evening, a furious arm'd Officer came to demand of me our County Subscription and Association, which I told him was never in my power to produce, so got rid of that Bully, then I hoped to hear no more from 'em in this mandatory way as to publick Matters. But the next day, after some thundering Rapps at my Door, came two other Officers, one seem'd a Scotch or ffrenchman, and the other a well dressed Englishman to demand of me my Horse, and in general to tell me there were several informations laid before their prince (which was the Appellation they distinguished him by) of my particular Disaffection towards him, and of being in conspiracy with several others to furnish the Duke of Devonshire with Horses, and that I must not only produce my own Horse secreted in or near the town as they were informed for the King and Dukes use, but give notice where others were to be met with, or else be instantly taken away prisoner. I told the Englishman (for the other was too outrageous to expostulate with) that four of my poor little Children were carried out of town for Refuge, and my Horse used on that occasion, but where they were fled to, could not tell. Upon that he said the reason was a good one, and forc'd the other Officer away with him. Soon after this an Hussar (as he called himself) came and took my Subscription Money, tho one half had been paid before, and a short time after that, Another Rascal called for the same money again, and forced me to send a Man with him, to the other Officer who recd. it. I was greatly afraid some Derby Incendiaries they had inlisted, or some others—Enemies to the Corporation, would have prompted these plunderers to have called for the Corporation Books, Charters, and Burgesses stamped Rolls in my custody for the destroying of the same, which would have brought great confusion to this Corporation and taken off all the legal Evidence (without otherwise remedied) for the support of a Borough Election, and so consequently have much affected the D. of Devonshire's interest in questions of that kind, but these Evidences have luckily escaped, and my staying here, I may say without Vanity was not a little contributory to it, but such another Trial would be intolerable. My Wife and I were not in Bed from Monday night till Friday, but constantly on the Watch to attend these Scoundrel Visitants, and to this case I can most truly and solemnly subscribe my Name and have every Article of it further verifyed if Desired.

WM. BATEMAN

19 May 1746."

This account by Mr. Bateman may shock those admirers of the Highlanders who are accustomed to dwell only on the heroic aspect of the Jacobite invasion of England. The account is certainly coarse and insular. But our ancestors were so exasperated by the constant anxieties to which they had been subjected ever since the capture of Edinburgh, and the defeat of the regular forces at Preston Pans, that we must make allowance for their state of mind. In similar circumstances we should doubtless feel precisely the same. Moreover, the Highlanders were regarded as barbarous and uncivilised people whose only virtue—if virtue it were— was an astonishing aptitude for war. The peace of England had been wantonly disturbed. The brutalities after Culloden can only be understood—that they can never be excused, goes without saying—if we realise the extent of the passionate hatred aroused by the Rebellion in the breasts of average Englishmen. The Duke of Cumberland was the darling of the nation, the subject of an idolatry which became blasphemous. The frontispiece of the *Gentleman's Magazine* for 1746, published just after the victory of Culloden, consists of an engraving of the Duke, with the incredible inscription: "Ecce Homo"!

On December 5th in Derby, Prince Charles Edward held that council of war which sealed the fate of the Rebellion. Realising that Cumberland was rapidly counter-marching to intercept any advance towards London, that General Wade was approaching through Yorkshire, and that the English Jacobites were not prepared to rise in arms, the Highland leaders—with the sole exception of the Prince— urged immediate retreat. Prince Charles Edward was forced to acquiesce, and on Friday, December 6th—the very day

on which London was in a state of consternation on learning
that the rebels had reached Derby—the retreat to Scotland
began. With what brilliant skill it was conducted by Lord
George Murray, how he defeated Cumberland's vanguard
at Clifton Moor, and how the whole Highland army
reached Scotland with the loss of hardly a man, is part of
military history. On December 20th—the Prince's birthday—the clans forded the Esk breast high, and for the
purposes of this account our parting view must be of them
playing their pipes and dancing their reels on the further
bank. Spell-bound we watch these heroic Highlanders
marching away to their native land, and to an immortal
place in the memories and the hearts of men!

Meanwhile the excursions and alarums, experienced by
the Duke of Devonshire's volunteer regiment while the
rebels were in Derby, are related in an honest and interesting
letter from Lord Hartington to Dr. Newcombe, written
from Chatsworth—now safe from invasion—on December
14th, 1745.

DEAR SR.

I received your kind Letter by the last post, and am much
obliged to you for the concern you express for my safety;
upon the Rebels first coming to Manchester my Father
assembled all the County Troops to Derby, we waited upon
the Duke at Litchfield to know if we could be of any
service, but His Royal Highness thought himself strong
enough, and I believe chose to trust the issue of a Battle
entirely to his old Troops, that were more to be depended
upon; when the Rebels came to Ashbourne which is ten

little miles from Derby, as it was impossible for us to think of resisting their whole force, we retired to Nottingham, we had some consultation there about maintaining a Pass over a small Brook between that Town and Derby, but after examination it did not prove tenable, so we marched the next day to Mansfield, where we had a false alarm that made us move our Quarters again. We had had flying reports most part of the Day that the Rebels were advancing our Way, which we had given no credit to, but on the contrary had sent a Captain with one Company to take Quarters in the Road towards Derby, in order to return there as soon as ye Highlanders had left it, imagining that they would have gone directly for London; just as it was growing dark our Captain returned and assur'd us that he had seen the Rebels to ye number of three or four thousand within two miles of the Town, and this being also confirmed by other advices, we thought it was *prudent* to get out of their way and we went to Retford, which brought us near the vanguard of Mr. Wade's army, but upon enquiry the Rebels had never stirred all that day from Derby except in small partys, to plunder and seize horses, which made the Country people drive off their Cattle in great Bodies which occasioned that alarm. As soon as ye Scotch were gone we returned to Derby, and I am surprised to find they have done so little damage. Most of the People of substance left the Town, by which means they did not get much money, their numbers, of all sorts including ye Country People that attended their Baggage and women and children, amounted to 7000, and about 5000 of them good fighting men; when they found they were to return they seemed much dejected, and every body seems to agree that they made a most contemptible appearance. The Duke

57

is gone after; whether he will be able to overtake them or not is some matter of doubt, we have heard nothing of them since Manchester, but we are in hourly expectation of some news. I am very much afraid lest they should get back to Scotland which may make it a tedious affair. I am very glad to hear the Duke [of Bridgewater or Chandos?] is recovered of the Measles. I beg my Compliments to Mrs. Newcome and His Grace, my service to Dr. Cheyney, pray let him know we are all well and that I intend to write to him very soon.

I am Dr. Sr.

Most sincerely yours

HARTINGTON.

Chatsworth
Dec. 14, 1745.

With the retreat of the rebel army the black cloud of anxiety which had so long hung over England was largely lifted: but not entirely. Invasion from the north was no longer to be feared: invasion from the south was hourly expected. This is made clear by two letters to the Duke of Devonshire in the Chatsworth MSS.—a lengthy one from the Duke of Newcastle, dated December 15th; a brief one from the Prime Minister, dated December 17th. As the Duke of Newcastle's letter contains a masterly review of the situation at home and abroad, I give it in full. But since Mr. Pelham so well maintains his pessimistic mood, it would be a pity to withhold from the reader the following characteristic passage in his letter:

"You have been much frightened in the North; we are a good deal so here now, the effects are terrible upon our credit: I pray for a speedy determination, for without that we are sure of a lingering death; with a stroke we have hopes of a speedy remedy."

The Duke of Newcastle's letter, dated from Whitehall, December 15th, 1745, is as follows:

MY LORD

I know your Grace's Goodness will excuse my not having sooner returned you Thanks for the Honor of your several Letters, and particularly those which gave the King the first Information of the Turn the Rebels took to Derby. Your Grace's attention and exactness in sending His Majesty, The Duke, and Marshal Wade such constant Accounts of the Motions of the Rebels was not only extremely agreeable to the King, but of infinite use for taking proper Measures upon Them. And indeed the Diligence used by the Duke in getting His Army so forward did, in all Probability, prevent the Rebels from coming towards London, which would have put everything here in the utmost Consternation, and Confusion.

By all our Advices from Dunkirk, the Preparations, which have been for some Time past making there for an Embarcation are now in such Forwardness that there is the greatest Reason to apprehend they will very soon attempt to put to sea. Their Destination seems to be some part of our Southern or Eastern Coast. But I hope, by the Blessing of God, they will be intercepted by the great number of Vessels that are stationed for that Purpose. By the last Advices, it looks as if they would not come with less than 12,000 men. They have a considerable Number of Vessels for Transports in Dunkirk, and have taken up a great Quantity of Fishing Boats, and small Boats, in order, as it is said, to fling over men into Sussex or Kent. We have a great Number of Ships of all sorts at sea, but are very poorly provided for our Defence at Land, not having, at present, above 6000 Men in and about London. For which Reason, we sent on Thursday Night for Ligonier to come up with all the Troops from Litchfield with the utmost Expedition, and for the Duke to follow with His, as soon as possible. His Royal Highness is only ordered to detach Campbell's and Sempil's and Four of the new raised Regiments of Foot, and with one Regiment of Dragoons, to join Marshal Wade's Army. The sending for the greatest part of the Duke's Army hither immediately was absolutely necessary for the Defence of the Capital against the intended Invasion; and at the same time I am afraid the Rebels will be able, either to remain in the North West Part of England, or to go into Scotland, and join the new Force which is getting together there, as they please. But Experience has showed how difficult it is to follow Them, or to get an head of Them.

The great Point now, with regard to the Rebels, must be, to make Marshl. Wade's Army as strong as possible; and to send it to Scotland, in order, if possible, to prevent the Rebels from being entirely Masters of that Kingdom. Wade Himself declines going to Scotland, on account of his age, and for other Reasons. I really think Him upon the whole, a very honest, and a very able Man; and I do not know where we shall be able to replace Him. Huske is talked of; and, in all respects would do very well; But he is only a Major General: However, Huske will go, and I believe my Lord Albermarle, and he will have the Command of the whole. Orders were sent on Friday last, for bringing over immediately the 6000 Hessians; and they are to go directly to Edinburgh. It is evident we have not Force enough, effectively to suppress the Rebellion at home, and to defend ourselves from the Attempts of our Enemies abroad.

All foreign Affairs are in as bad a way as possible: The Dutch in the utmost distress, from our having recalled all our Troops and will be more so, when they shall hear We have sent for the Hessians also. But that is a necessary Step; and I heartily wish it had been taken a month ago when I advised it.

The Queen of Hungary, from that fatal Obstinacy, which attends her, has now recalled all her Troops from the Rhine; and some of the few, which she had in Flanders; (and I think some of those which We paid;) in order to pursue her Chimerical Project against the King of Prussia; towards which she has hitherto miscarried in every step that she has taken; And by this last, she has entirely abandoned the Empire and the Netherlands. But, at present, all my attention is confined to this Island; which, I think, continues in the utmost Danger.

My Brother, I conclude, sent you word of the remarkable Behaviour of Mr. Pitt, the last day the House sat; whereby He seems to have made all further Correspondence extremely difficult. The Duke of Bedford, and Lord Gower, continue as zealously united with us as possible.

As the Rebels are now got quite clear of Derbyshire, and on their Return towards Scotland; I hope your Grace will think of returning immediately to London, where your Presence is extremely wanted on many accounts: and I am persuaded you will take care to have constant Accounts of everything that shall pass in the Country.

As to the case of Mr. Heathcote, your Grace will please to give such Directions as you shall think proper; and your

Grace will assure Sir Nathaniel Curzon, that, whatever your Grace and he shall think right, will be extremely approved by the King.

> I am with great Truth, and Respect
> My Lord
> Your Grace's
> most Obedient
> humble Servant
> HOLLES NEWCASTLE.

In another month's time the fear of invasion from France had ceased to haunt London, and Horace Walpole, writing to Horace Mann from Arlington Street on January 17th, 1746, was able to report: " The French invasion is laid aside; we are turning our hands to war again upon the continent."[1] The crisis of 1745 had come to an end. It is true that the rebel army inflicted a decisive defeat on the regular army commanded by General Hawley at Falkirk on the very day that Horace Walpole was writing so cheerfully[2] to his friend. But this defeat, however humiliating to English pride, could not stop the solemn march of events towards the field of Culloden. And with the last months of the Rebellion we are not concerned here. Our purpose has been to show, from the intimate records preserved at Chatsworth, how continuous was the atmosphere of crisis in town and country in the six months from July to December 1745: above all, to convey some vivid sense of that

[1] Horace Walpole's *Letters*, Paget Toynbee edition, Vol. II, p. 169.
[2] "What a despicable affair is a rebellion upon the defensive!" he says in this same letter.

"unimaginable touch of time" which lingers in old manuscripts as we turn over the leaves. Yes! The Duke of Newcastle is agitated, and Mr. Pelham is depressed; Lord Hartington's black mare still waits for him at Derby; the Duchess of Devonshire's hogshead of madeira sets out from town on Monday; Lady Charlotte Boyle's company is extremely innocent and agreeable; the Duke of Devonshire is very much what he always was and, doubtless, always will be—the faithful friend of his countrymen in the Midlands first and foremost, and in the second place the good colleague of Ministers—supplying the indispensable elements of calm, of solid sense, and constant loyalty. As for those "devilish good marchers," the Highlanders, the Duke will allow himself a final flick of irony in a letter from Chatsworth to Lord Hartington (back again in London) on New Year's Day, 1746:

"I think those countries, that have been visited by the Rebels, do not desire to see them again."

Chapter Two

GENERAL GORDON[1]

The life of General Gordon was so extraordinary, his personality so compelling, that we find ourselves almost daunted when we think about him. If you are a sceptic and disinclined to believe in miracles, and if you wish to remain in that state of mind, you would be well advised not to study the life of General Gordon. For, if you pursue the thread of his life, you will find very soon that he is not dead at all, that you are compelled to believe in immortality, and that the be-all and the end-all here is moonshine. If, on the other hand, you are perfectly prepared to meet a mystic, and to walk quietly with the disciples to Emmaus, you will find yourself violently startled, and your walk will not be tranquil. On the other hand, at the end of the journey, you will realise that you have arrived, and that your heart burned within you on the way.

For, from that powerful and beautiful personality there is no escape. You may think that once the spear has entered his body on that early morning of January 26th, 1885, that once the head has been severed from the shoulders and shown in mockery to Slatin Pasha—the eyes half open, and

[1] This essay was written as a paper for "The Makers," a literary society of St. Edmund Hall, Oxford, and was read on February 28th, 1933, shortly after the Gordon centenary.

the mouth perfectly natural—that at last you will speak to him no more. It is not so. And finally you cry out: "I fear thee, Ancient Mariner." But instantly the answer comes:

> *"Be calm, thou Wedding-Guest!*
> *'Twas not those souls that fled in pain,*
> *Which to their corses came again,*
> *But a troop of spirits blest."*

It may reasonably be asked: "But how did you become at all acquainted with General Gordon, and why do you speak of him in this almost agitated way?" I frankly answer that General Gordon was killed three years before I was born, that though I studied history at the university, the enthralling history of the latter half of the nineteenth century was hardly taught in my time—so strange are the vagaries of educational method—and that, till 1918, Gordon was merely a name, though a noble one, vaguely associated with China, with the slave-trade and with Khartoum.

Then, in 1918, Lytton Strachey's *Eminent Victorians* was published, and as soon as one had read the essay on Gordon one understood in a flash why his name was not only eminent, but pre-eminent. Since that time I have probed and read as much as might be about Gordon. But the literature is enormous. It is the fashion of the moment to decry Strachey, and particularly to revile him for that last essay in *Eminent Victorians*. The writers on the Gordon centenary seem simply to have remembered the brandy-bottle passages, and to have forgotten everything else. It really shows how wicked we all are. We remember what is

evil and forget what is good. But the truth is that when
Strachey, misled by a hostile and unattractive creature
called Colonel Chaillé-Long,[1] suggested that Gordon over-
indulged in stimulants, he simply "wrote himself down."
For we know on good eighteenth-century authority, and
no wiser apophthegm was ever uttered: "that no man was
ever written down, but by himself." For my part I never
believed the Strachey drink suggestion. It seemed utterly
incompatible with the life and character of Gordon, as
brilliantly related by Strachey himself. To me the really
extraordinary and interesting thing is, that so sceptical a
person as Lytton Strachey should have been, in effect,
completely overcome by Gordon. He pretends to scoff at
his biblical studies, and he tries to believe at moments
that Gordon was more an *enfant terrible* of Victorian times
than anything else. But we are not deceived. That is simply
the Bloomsbury façade. We enter the house, make our way
to the study, and find Lytton Strachey at his desk, writing
with a hand which visibly trembles with emotion. He looks
over his shoulder rather nervously, as though he almost
heard again Gordon's rapid step behind him, and then he
suddenly finds himself writing sentences about "the
scatheless equanimity of a Demi-god."

It was the same with the sceptics of his own generation.
They, too, realised that there was something outside
ordinary standards of human measurement in Gordon.

[1] Dr. B. M. Allen in his outstanding book *Gordon and the Sudan*
(Macmillan, 1931) has finally disposed of Col. C. Long. This book has
placed all students of Gordon's career deeply in Dr. Allen's debt.

"Poor fellow!" wrote Huxley, when he heard what he called the hideous news of the Khartoum catastrophe—

"I wonder if he has entered upon the larger sphere of action which he told me was reserved for him in case of such a trifling accident as death. Of all the people I have met with in my life, he and Darwin are the two in whom I have found something bigger than ordinary humanity—an unequalled simplicity and directness of purpose—a sublime unselfishness."[1]

Lord Wolseley, who had known Gordon throughout his military career, beginning with their service as young officers at the siege of Sebastopol, wrote of him ten years after his death with poignant and soldier-like simplicity: "I always felt, and more than ever feel now, that I was never worthy to pipe-clay his belt for him."[2] But the cloud of witnesses stretches out infinitely—some still living—who speak with the same voice. Let us, therefore, set out ourselves in search of that pilgrim who once journeyed so far afield in Europe, in Asia and in Africa, who looked upon this life as a mere interlude, who hoped to meet death in the Crimea, and after thirty years of persistent pursuit came up with the mysterious angel in Khartoum.

It is the exception rather than the rule for the explanation of genius to be found in ancestry—perhaps because in so many cases the ancestral record is not sufficiently complete. In Gordon's case the ancestors seem to explain the outward

[1] Quoted from a letter in *The Times* sent by Mr. Leonard Huxley, February 2nd, 1933.
[2] *Gordon and the Sudan*, by Dr. B. M. Allen, p. 100.

and visible, but not the inward and spiritual. On the Gordon side his father, grandfather and great-grandfather were all soldiers; on his mother's side he came of a great merchant-shipping family, Samuel Enderby being almost a Lord Inchcape of the eighteenth century, sending his ships into all seas. But the pedigree compilers have not been able to trace the paternal side beyond Gordon's great-grandfather, David Gordon. David, contrary to all one's natural expectations, is found fighting in the '45 in the army of George II, and not, as almost all the Gordons were, for Prince Charles Edward. Therefore, it is not absolutely certain that Gordon was descended from the great clan, though all the inferences and traditions would seem to point that way. He himself thought he was nearly connected with the Gordons of Glenbucket.[1] Gordon's father rose to be a Lieutenant-General, and three of his sons, including Charles George, in due course entered the Army.

At sixteen, Gordon entered Woolwich, and after a strenuous four years qualified as a Second Lieutenant in the Royal Engineers. His twenty odd years so far have not been particularly notable, but already the traits of his character are coming out. Through his mother and his eldest sister, who were deeply evangelical, Gordon is introduced to the literature which is the foundation of his life. From some bygone ancestor, perhaps a wild, ferocious Highlander in the remote mists and mountains of Scotland, he inherited an obstreperousness of disposition, bordering

[1] Letter of Lord Huntly in *The Times*, February 1st, 1933; see also Dr. Bullock's *Times* letter of January 30th, 1933.

almost on blank insubordination. Hitting a fellow cadet on the head with a broomstick was thought to be over-doing it even in 1851, and the military authorities at Woolwich were seriously displeased. We sympathise more with his intense distaste for examinations. Not long before his death he had a dream: "I had a fearful dream last night," he wrote, "I was back at the Academy, and had to pass an examination." Ah! How many of us have had the same nightmare, and woken up in the same cold sweat!

In 1854, Gordon was stationed at Pembroke and found himself already in the grip of those two emotions which dominated his life—a profound religious experience, and a longing to be sent out to that part of the world, at this time the Crimea, where fighting and death were in full possession of the field. On Easter Day, 1854, he received the Sacrament for the first time. He had not been confirmed, and never was confirmed. His religion, like his life, was absolutely his own. Authority and discipline imposed from without he hardly endured, or endured only to the minimum extent. His own self-discipline was intense. His body was subjected to every hardship. His mind, though completely submissive to God, he found very insubordinate to himself, despite great efforts to curb its enormous insolence. Two of his brothers were already fighting in the Crimea. Gordon thought it was a great shame that his mother should try and divert him to the security of Corfu, particularly since, as he afterwards told his beloved sister Augusta—how that name wafts us back to the Victorian drawing-room—he hoped to get killed.

Gordon now indulged in a little wire-pulling, and managed to have himself ordered to the Crimea in December of this same year. We have not time to linger over this period of Gordon's career. We must content ourselves with a flying glimpse of the scenes of sound and fury and extremities of human endurance, scenes on which Gordon enters with almost an uncanny calm of mind. Men are frozen to death, the very ink in which he dips his pen for his letters home freezes as he writes, then the spring begins to come and the crocuses break through the stubborn earth, and with the spring and summer, endless attack and counter-attack, men mown down like flies, mines and counter-mines, Sebastopol at last taken—the Russians retiring and abandoning to the Allies there, as Gordon puts it, "nothing but rubbish and fleas." He finds all the fighting "indescribably exciting." The war ends in the spring of 1856, and Gordon spends the next four years in the wilds of Bessarabia and Armenia, delimiting frontiers, with one or two returns home in between. He can be seen cutting his way through impenetrable forests, climbing up the Armenian mountains, including the immemorial and immense Mount Ararat, now plunged in limitless solitudes, and now watching in the ancient cities—Jews, Turks, Greeks, and Russians, Caucasian princesses and the lovely Gourelians. The Gourelians at this time were being regularly kidnapped to supply the insatiable demand of the wealthy Turks for slaves, and for harems.

In the year 1860, Gordon, now a Captain in the Royal Engineers, and already, at the age of twenty-seven, almost

71

a veteran in military and cosmopolitan experiences, finds himself with the British and French forces in China in the interlude of a brief commercial war. The war itself was almost over when Gordon arrived. In the autumn he was in Peking, the city celestial and sordid, though the sordidness is forgotten under the magic of such names as the ancient Temple of Heaven, the Temple of Earth, and the Golden Fish-ponds; forgotten in the kaleidoscopic vision of towering walls, palaces, and pavilions, of shops the colour of the rainbow—lit up at night with the bright authentic lanterns of our childhood, and with torches, of streets crowded with humanity, with curious vehicles of all sorts and sizes, and with camels and mules and men carrying the merchandise of remote provinces.

And now, as the Chinese War was drawing to a close, and preliminaries of peace were beginning to be discussed, a dreadful incident occurred. The representatives of the British Envoy, though protected by a flag of truce, were seized by the war-lords of the Chinese Army and subjected to maltreatment not far, if at all distinguishable, from torture. Several of the captives died. As a punishment for this treacherous and dastardly crime, the British and French forces destroyed the exquisite Summer Palace of the Emperors, eight miles north-west of Peking. The British Envoy who ordered this act was the eighth Lord Elgin, a man of wide experience—he had been Governor-General of Canada and was afterwards Viceroy of India—and of many virtues. His action is the more extraordinary as he wholeheartedly, in his journals, condemns the looting which the

French, in particular, indulged in as the allied forces advanced on Peking. He was particularly shocked by the partial pillage of the Summer Palace itself on October 7th, and on that day observes: "War is a hateful business. The more one sees of it, the more one detests it." But his mind seems to have hardened and become embittered in the days following when he heard of the death of two of the English prisoners, and of the cruel fate of others of the captives. So on October 18th he ordered the Summer Palace, where the criminal maltreatment of the prisoners had taken place, to be burned. In his despatch of October 25th, he says that he examined various alternative methods of inflicting punishment for the crime on the captives, and finally decided that destruction of the Summer Palace was "the least objectionable of the several courses open to me, unless I could have reconciled it to my sense of duty to suffer the crime which had been committed to pass practically unavenged. I had reason, moreover, to believe that it was an act which was calculated to produce a greater effect in China, and on the Emperor, than persons who look on from a distance may suppose." In the Chinese proclamation which Lord Elgin had posted on the walls, he says that the Palace "was burnt as a punishment inflicted on the Emperor for the violation of his word, and the act of treachery to a flag of truce."[1] It is odd to reflect that Lord Elgin was the son of the preserver of the Parthenon Marbles. Gordon, who was compelled to take part in this

[1] *Letters and Journals of James, 8th Earl of Elgin*, edited by T. Walrond (1872), pp. 353–67.

holocaust, wrote of it with a vividness which reveals his horror:

"You can scarcely imagine the beauty and magnificence of the palaces we burnt," he says. "It made one's heart sore to burn them; in fact, those palaces were so large, and we were so pressed for time, that we could not plunder them carefully. Quantities of gold ornaments were burned, considered as brass. It was wretchedly demoralising work for an army. Everybody was wild for plunder. You would scarcely conceive the tremendous devastation the French have committed. The throne room was lined with ebony, carved in a marvellous way. There were huge mirrors of all shapes and kinds, clocks, watches, musical boxes with puppets on them, magnificent china of every description, heaps and heaps of silk of all colours, embroidery, and as much splendour and civilisation as you would see at Windsor; carved ivory screens, coral screens, large amounts of treasure. The French have smashed everything in the most wanton way. It was a scene of utter desolation which passes my description."[1]

It is at least a consolation to reflect, after reading such an account, that this Vandal-like revenge was about to be atoned for by a young officer in the British Army, whose suppression of the Taiping Rebellion was the means of saving tens of thousands of poor souls, and of rendering incalculable services to the Emperor of China, and to civilisation.

The Taiping Rebellion had broken out in 1850 under the

[1] Boulger's *Life of General Gordon*, Vol. I, pp. 45–6.

leadership of a fanatic called Hung. Hung, having failed to pass an examination in 1837—the Chinese passion for examinations actually, it seems, exceeds our own—sought consolation in religious speculations, which ended in his believing that he was the younger brother of Jesus, was the Heavenly King, and was the evangelist of Taiping, the reign of peace. Followers gathered round him, the Chinese Government endeavoured to suppress the movement, failed to do so and found themselves faced with a first-class rebellion in the very heart of the richest province of the Empire. The cities and villages in the delta of the Yang-tse, the greatest river of China, navigable for more than a thousand miles, were captured one after another by the Taiping forces. As early as 1853, Nanking, the ancient capital of China, fell before the Heavenly King's hordes. The real character of the apostle of peace was revealed in the smoke of burning villages and the sack of cities. When Nanking was captured, ten thousand Manchus were murdered, though they had been promised their lives if they surrendered. The magnificent, many-coloured Porcelain Tower of the ancient Emperors of the Ming Dynasty, more than three hundred feet high, lighted with over a hundred lanterns and made musical with a multitude of bells, was destroyed.

At length the Imperial troops began to make headway against the rebel Taipings. But the war of 1860 with France and England was fatal to their success, and the old chaos and brutalities were violently revived. Shanghai was threatened. The foreign merchants combined with the local mandarins, and a cosmopolitan force of somewhat

75

ruffianly character was raised. An American named Ward, assisted by another American named Burgevine, commanded this force. It was at first successful, but soon met with disaster and was disbanded. Ward, with great energy, raised a larger force, consisting mainly of Chinese, officered by Europeans, and during the next two years this force achieved so many successes that an Imperial edict bestowed upon it the title of the "Ever-victorious Army." In September of 1862, however, Ward was killed. Burgevine and an English officer named Holland were successively appointed to the command, and successively discovered to be incompetent. Finally, in March 1863, when the Ever-victorious Army was in a state of disintegration and mutiny after various defeats, General Staveley, who commanded the British forces in Shanghai, pressed the Chinese Government to appoint his brother-in-law, Captain Gordon, to the command. General Staveley, who had assisted the Ever-victorious Army in keeping the Taipings at a wholesome distance from Shanghai, was well acquainted with his relative's abilities. For Gordon had for some time past been carrying out under the nose of the Taipings an accurate survey of the network of water-ways and the location of the cities and villages in the Yang-tse delta.

Gordon at once discussed his plan of campaign with Li Hung Chang, the Imperial Governor of the province, assured him that complete victory would be secured in eighteen months, and forthwith, with a rapidity and energy which can only be described as dæmonic, entered upon his task.

His determination to end the Rebellion with all possible
speed was doubtless influenced by his intense sympathy
for the poor villagers whose lives were one long nightmare,
even if they escaped with life: and the numbers who perished
were incalculable. "We are all impressed," wrote Gordon
to his mother, "with the utter misery and wretchedness of
these poor people."[1]

The country in which the campaign was fought to a finish
within considerably less than eighteen months was a network of rivers, canals, creeks, and lakes. The soil was of
great richness, growing every variety of crop, while the
trees which fed the gold-weaving silk-worms flourished
abundantly. The cities of this region, headed by the great
city of Soo-chow, centre of the silk industry, and famous
for its loveliness and wealth, were surrounded by crenel-
lated walls, with towers at intervals, and gateways opening
to the four points of the compass. Ditches, moats and canals
were frequent around and within the city walls.[2]

It is beyond the compass of this essay to describe the
campaign, and the triumphant capture of city after city
whose very names sound like a chime of pleasant, jangling
bells—Foo-Shan, Chanzu, Tait-san, Quin-san, Soo-chow,
Yesing, Liyang, Kong-ying, Chang-chu-fu.

Spell-bound we can only watch Gordon with his bodyguard of three hundred, in uniforms of blue faced with
scarlet, the remainder of his force of three thousand in

[1] Quoted in H. E. Wortham's *Gordon: An Intimate Portrait*, p. 69.
[2] Sir W. Butler's *Charles George Gordon*, ch. iii, contains an excellent
account of the character of the country in which the campaign was fought.

green—the colour and rapidity of motion remind us of a kingfisher—darting up and down rivers and canals in his steamer the *Hyson* accompanied by a flotilla of boats and junks, ceaselessly chasing flying Taipings, and surprising their cities and strongholds by suddenness of manœuvre and complete unexpectedness of approach. Extraordinary scenes pass before our eyes—the rebels defending their city walls with desperation amid the barbaric clashing of gongs and blowing of horns, intermixed with gun and rifle fire and the throwing of stink-pots and brickbats; Gordon advancing with his cane—which came to be called the wand of victory—or waving his battle flag, or suddenly picking up a naked Chinese baby on the canal bank and carrying it in his arms as he directed the brilliant operation at Quin-san; Gordon threatened by the stark mutiny of certain N.C.O.s who threaten to blow their officers to pieces, parading the mutineers, and himself seizing the ringleader and having him shot instantly by his bodyguard: then, after the capture of the central stronghold of Soo-chow, we see him in uncontrollable grief and rage resigning his command because the Wangs—the rebel leaders—having surrendered on his promise that their lives would be spared, are ruthlessly decapitated by the Imperial troops; "the destiny of China is at the present moment in the hands of Gordon more than of any other man," wrote the wise Robert Hart at this moment of crisis; Gordon at last relents, resumes the command with the usual victory at first, and then suffers defeat at Kintang where he is also wounded; he is defeated again; it makes no difference to

his serene self-confidence; the whirlwind campaign is continued and ends with the rebel rout at Waisso, and the
capture on May 11th, 1864, of the stronghold of Chang-
chu-fu.[1]

"Your career during the last two years of your residence
in the East," wrote the foreign merchants and inhabitants
of Shanghai in an address of gratitude to Gordon at the
conclusion of the Taiping Rebellion, "has been, so far
as we know, without parallel in the history of the intercourse
of foreign nations with China." The Imperial Government
bestowed upon him the highest honours in their power:
he was made a Field Marshal and a Mandarin of the
Order of the Yellow Jacket, while a special gold medal
was struck in his honour. Money he declined to take. "We
do not know what to do," wrote the Regent of China,
Prince Kung, to the British Minister. "He will not receive
money from us, and we have already given him every
honour which it is in the power of the Emperor to bestow;
but as these can be of little value in his eyes, I have brought
you this letter, and ask you to give it to the Queen of
England."[2]

The English Government thereupon bestowed upon him
a C.B. They had already promoted him to be a Lieutenant-
Colonel. We smile as we read. Such modest recognition
by the Home Government is curious, particularly as *The
Times* in a leader of August 5th, 1864, on his Chinese

[1] Mr. H. E. Wortham's *Intimate Portrait* deals admirably with the
Chinese phase of Gordon's career.

[2] See Hake's *Chinese Gordon*, Vol. I, ch. viii.

79

services had explained to English readers what Gordon had done, and how he had effected all this, "by the power of his arms, and the terror of his name." But, after all, worldly honours are neither here nor there in the case of a person like Gordon. As Pitt had observed in 1798, when someone criticised the Government for only giving Nelson a barony after the battle of the Nile:

"Admiral Nelson's fame would be co-equal with the British name; and it would be remembered that he had obtained the greatest naval victory on record, when no man would think of asking whether he had been created a baron, a viscount or an earl."[1]

Gordon's own view of his services was summed up in a letter to his mother on the eve of the fall of Chang-chu-fu:

"I know I shall leave China as poor as I entered it, but with the knowledge that through my weak instrumentality upwards of 80 to 100,000 lives have been spared. I want no further satisfaction than this." And again later, "I think if my proceedings sank into oblivion it would be the better for everyone."

He certainly took every step possible to mortal man, not only to escape publicity, but to busy himself in humdrum obscurity. In September of 1865 the War Office, without apparently any conscious attempt to perpetrate a joke, entrusted Gordon with the work of superintending the erection of five forts at the mouth of the Thames. Gordon soon reported that the money would be wasted. The superior

[1] Quoted in Southey's *Life of Nelson*.

authorities disagreed: the work must be done. So Gordon spent six peaceful years at Gravesend.

The Gravesend period of Gordon's career is in some ways the most significant. He himself looked back to it as the happiest time of any in his life. Ambition—and he was in reality intensely ambitious—was suppressed, and we know from the recent testimony of Sir Bindon Blood[1] that he resolutely rejected the advice of his brother officers to apply for a transfer to the Indian Army which then seemed the only sure path to military promotion. No! If he was passed over or forgotten, well and good. Meanwhile he would seek to interpret the divine message with increased intensity. He pored over the pages of the Bible and prayed—had he not prayed his soldiers to victory in China? And all around him were the poor and needy. His duty became clear.

In order to understand Gordon's religious views it is necessary to read the letters to his sister which were published after his death, and went through three editions within two months of publication. It is impossible to convey any adequate idea of the singular character of this book. It seems as though Gordon were still talking in the room—with the characteristic vivacity, the eagerness and the oddity. The eye and the expression, which, his friend Mrs. Freese observed, "might have been a thousand years old," are fixed upon you and then suddenly cast down as though he had forgotten you and himself and everything but the indwelling God. For that idea of the indwelling God was

[1] Sir Bindon Blood in his ninety-first year broadcast an admirable address on Gordon on January 28th, 1933.

his central belief which sustained him in all perplexities. In a paper which he wrote at Gravesend, one of several which Miss Gordon—Augusta—included with his published letters, he says:

"I believe there is a spiritual child of God in everyone, which is the true self, and was with us in Christ before the world began, and will be with us in the eternal future." And again: "I am more than ever convinced that the secret of happiness and holiness is in the indwelling of God."

It was a verse in St. John's First Epistle which made this profound impression upon him. "Keep in view," he says —with that pleasing evangelical simplicity which wove texts into the pattern of everyday talk—"keep in view 1 John iv. 15; it has in few words the great secret of the new life." You look up the text and read: "Whosoever shall confess that Jesus is the Son of God, God dwelleth in him, and he in God." To Gordon there were two entirely separate natures always in conflict, the carnal and the spiritual. Some people during their earthly existence were "born again"; others were so sinful that only death could destroy the carnal creature and release the spiritual to its abiding place with God. His creed is magnificently generous and optimistic: there is no place for purgatory or torment in it. "Endeavour to realise the completeness of salvation to *all* men; know that God rules all things, even evil." Then, developing his ideas, and taking account of the worst of men and women, he asks: "What do we know of the influences to which they have been submitted, influences which it was not in their power to avoid, such as their birth, bringing up? . . . We may rest assured that God loves us, loves us all, infinitely." As for sects, join none, though there may be truth in all. Throughout his life he clung passionately to his belief in the absolute salvation of all men. No one would be cast out.

No man ever set to work to do good in a more direct and practical way than Gordon. He accepted the social system as he found it, and, reading the Gospels, he did not discover that they preached any revolutionary political doctrine. "We do not find Him," he said, "in any way taking the part of the poor against the rich individually. He pointed out the fallacy of the pious rich in thinking they fulfilled the law while they neglected their brethren."

Relatively to his neighbours, Gordon in his pleasant house, Fort House, with its even more pleasant garden, was rich. It is impossible to give any adequate account of his Gravesend good works, but after considering the means he adopted to help the poor and needy it becomes clear that, if his example were at all widely followed by us to-day, the social problem would be transformed. Teaching in the Ragged School, keeping open house, particularly for the boys belonging to the fishing fleets, making his garden into a resting place for the old, visiting the infirmary, reading to the sick, praying by the bedside of the dying, sending children to the Zoo for a treat, or to the sea if they were ill, paying arrears of rent to save the furniture of a poverty-stricken home, finding places for the boys whom he had rescued from destitution, sending his Chinese gold medal—

83

after he had erased the inscription—to the Lancashire Famine Fund, starting a night school in his house which was so frequented that almost every room was occupied, of such a kind were the activities of Colonel Gordon at Gravesend.[1] The Presbyterian parson there was about to go away for his holiday, but did not like to leave a poor woman who was dying from some fatal disease. He mentioned the case to Gordon, and on his return from his holiday he found that Gordon had visited her every day, and had comforted her on her death-bed.

"I think our life," wrote Gordon to his sister, on December 28th, 1870, "is summed up in patient waiting and in being content with the evil of the day. Night soon comes, and with it comes rest." Four years later, on December 21st, 1874, he is writing to Augusta from the heart of Equatorial Africa, where he was struggling with incredible hardships and obstacles: "What an extraordinary and mysterious thing that there should be such difficulties with these sources of the Nile! . . . Make what arrangements you will, and yet you will find it blocked time after time." And then after some admirably original remarks on the divine governance of the universe he ends up his letter:

"There, I have written enough for to-day, and will go and 'worrit' the Arabs! but with the remembrance that, looking deeply, it is very little real importance if they do what I tell them or not—not that I tell them *that*. I have a

[1] I base this brief summary of Gordon's good works on a little book, *The Life and Work of General Gordon at Gravesend*, by W. E. Lilley, published in 1885.

beautiful meershaum mouthpiece bought from Marno for Mr. Hansall, who happily for me does not smoke. It is a splendid bit, and I have accepted it. Do you know date-stones will give fruit-bearing trees or shrubs three years after planting?"[1]

Gordon had left Gravesend in the autumn of 1871. After two years of special commission work on the Danube he had been invited by the Khedive of Egypt, Ismail, to carry on the work, begun on behalf of the Khedive by Sir Samuel Baker in 1869, of opening up and annexing the Equatorial provinces to Egypt, and of suppressing the slave-trade. A recent writer, Pierre Crabitès, in his book *Gordon, the Sudan and Slavery*, has done tardy justice to the Khedive Ismail. Ismail may have been grossly extravagant in financial matters—Lord Cromer's *Modern Egypt* contains a weighty diatribe against him—but he had great ideas, and it was his plain intention to civilise the remote southern regions bordering on Egypt, and to suppress the slave-trade with its foul barbarities.[2]

Gordon, early in February 1874, arrived in Cairo and was made Governor-General of the Equator. Under this vague term were comprised great regions of Africa stretching from a point some four hundred miles south of Khartoum down to the Equatorial lakes, regions so far explored by white men only in patches. The trade of these regions was ivory, ebony and slaves, and the slaves, captured from the primitive African tribes, were the carriers of the ivory and

[1] *Letters to his Sister*, p. 40 and pp. 95–7.
[2] *Gordon, the Sudan and Slavery*, by P. Crabitès, ch. iv.

the ebony before they were themselves sold to the Arab, the Egyptian, and the Turk. It was Gordon's central idea, which he had formed before arriving in Cairo, that the ultimate and only lasting solution of the slave problem was to open out the country.

"My ideas are," he said, in a letter of November 17th, 1873, to his sister, "to open the country by getting the steamers on to the lakes, by which time I should know the promoters of the slave trade and could ask the Khedive to seize them."[1]

By February 1874 he had worked out his plans with the Khedive, and the Khedivial instructions—doubtless drafted by Gordon himself—directed him to establish a Government monopoly in the ivory-trade with a view to suppressing slave-raids, to promote friendly relations with the native tribes, and to set up a line of posts on the Nile so that there might be direct communication with Khartoum.[2]

As we read the story of the next seven years of Gordon's life we are again impressed with a sense—as during the Taiping period—of a being above and outside ordinary standards of human measurement. Our sense of the magnitude of his achievement is not lessened by the knowledge that much of his work was to be completely obliterated during the sixteen years of anarchy and outrage which followed the Mahdi's rebellion. If the mitigation of human

[1] *Letters to his Sister*, pp. 90–1.
[2] See Pierre Crabitès: *Gordon, the Sudan and Slavery*, pp. 28–30, where the full document is given.

suffering ought to be the supreme moral aim of power,
then Gordon's life is almost unique among men. Taking the
African period of his life alone, we see an enormous redemp-
tion of the down-trodden and tortured during the successive
periods of his Equatorial and Sudan rule, that is to say
during the years 1873 to 1880. If we look beyond the
catastrophe of 1884–5, when the fall of Khartoum sealed
the fate of an area almost as great as Europe, till Kitchener
re-conquered the Sudan in 1898, we are driven to the
conclusion that Gordon's example, his suffering and his
death, were the means of shortening the intermediate
period of chaos and calamity. Lord Cromer, no friendly
witness to Gordon, writing in the second volume of his
Modern Egypt, admits that, if he had been asked in 1886,
he would have conjectured that the Sudan would not be
re-conquered for another twenty-five years from that date.
The re-conquest undertaken in 1896–8 by Gordon's
brother officer, Lord Kitchener, was undertaken then for
a variety of reasons. But among them, according to Lord
Cromer, was the popular feeling that "Gordon should be
avenged." And he concludes his otherwise admirable
chapter on the re-conquest of Khartoum by some rather
jejune observations on the importance of not ignoring
national sentiment in these matters.[1] Mr. George Trevelyan,

[1] Lord Cromer's *Modern Egypt*, Vol. II, ch. xxxii. See also Mr. Winston
Churchill's *The River War*, p. 173: "The diplomatist said: 'It is to please
the Triple Alliance.' The politician said: 'It is to triumph over the
Radicals.' The polite person said: 'It is to restore the Khedive's rule in
the Sudan.' But the man in the street, and there are many men in many
streets, said: 'It is to avenge General Gordon.' "

in his *British History in the Nineteenth Century*, dealing with the crisis of 1884–5, sums up its effect as follows: "The conscious Imperialism of the national sentiment in the following generation received an impulse from the fate of Gordon. An idealist, a soldier and a Christian hero, he supplied to the popular imagination whatever was lacking in Disraeli as the patron saint of the new religion of Empire."[1] We might perhaps add that to the present generation the main importance of the re-conquest of the Sudan lies, not in any solace to Imperialistic sentiment, but in the knowledge that millions of defenceless souls have been rescued from unspeakable sufferings. That, in Gordon's eyes, would have been the first and final justification for the Omdurman campaign. "I declare solemnly," he said in 1877, "that I would give my life willingly to save the sufferings of these people."

It is now necessary after this deliberate digression— for it is sometimes helpful to fly forwards in order to look back on the course of history—to return to Equatorial Africa. For three years we must dive into pestilential swamps and endure what De Quincey calls, "the cancerous kisses of crocodiles"; thereafter we enter, almost without rest, into vast expanses of Sudan desert, the sun scorching down as we pursue a remote speck on the horizon— Gordon whirling away out of sight on his solitary camel.

Towards the end of March of 1874 the Governor-General of the Equator was rapidly approaching his dominion as he steamed down the White Nile: in particular

[1] Trevelyan's *British History in the Nineteenth Century*, pp. 388–9.

he took note of the animals—the storks who laughed at
him in the moonlight, "the crocodiles lying interlaced
on the few rocks, with their mouths, garnished with teeth,
wide open. Hippopotamuses were also active. Troops
of monkeys were not far distant. They came down to drink,
with very long tails stuck up straight like swords over their
backs."[1] Also there were herds of coal-black buffaloes.
Rats, of course, were constant companions, and he describes
them as "circusing about everywhere, and I fear that the
older ones eat the younger members of their families, for
there are great outcries at night, with lamentations and woe,
and I found part of a young rat eaten by an older one, and
the remainder left for my benefit—a delicate attention!"[2]
But all these creatures were almost charming companions
compared with the terrible scourge of insects, the sand-
flies, the harvest-bugs and, above all, the malarial mosquitoes
which swarmed in thousands. At Gondokoro, in September
of 1874, almost every member of his small European staff
succumbed to fever, or nearly succumbed. And the rain
poured down relentlessly in sheets and in torrents, while
Gordon paddled about in his tent, attending to the sick.
For himself he had no fear, sustained by his absolute belief
in God. Certainly, one had need of an enormous faith
to struggle against the vast accumulation of difficulties
and thwartings: for these flowed down upon one as relentlessly as the great river, the ultimate reaches of which had
not been explored. Gordon prayed that the Nile might—

[1] *Gordon in Central Africa,* edited by Geo. Birckbeck Hill.
[2] *Letters to his Sister,* pp. 93-4.

despite rocks and rapids—be found to be navigable to the great lakes. But in this he was doomed to disappointment. So with a strange awe we look back at him and watch him toiling away.

Slave-girls and spirits are the pay vouchsafed by the Cairo authorities for the Egyptian troops in Gondokoro. That must be stopped at once. New stations must be established, so as to ensure rapidity of communication on the thousand-mile stretches of the Equatorial Nile. The Nile must cease to be the route for the slavers. But the slavers are incredibly wily. Innocent looking boats come down to the stations piled with wood. You lift up the wood and find nearly a hundred black woolly heads huddled beneath. These poor souls are forthwith released and are settled happily at one of the new stations, as free tillers of the soil. Then there is treachery to be faced: suddenly Gordon's tent is surrounded by some dark warriors whose chief advances with a club. Gordon takes up his gun and simply orders the chief to be gone, and he goes. Or one sees the romantic spectacle of 500 coal-black natives arriving at the new station of Lado, bearing ivory, now a Government monopoly. Further and further up the great river, praying the *nuggars* up the rapids with ropes breaking and the boats whirled down again! And the natives become suspicious at one point and dislike the look of the snorting steamer, the *Khedive*. One of Gordon's best lieutenants, Linant, goes out to overawe them, is ambushed with forty men, and all are speared save one. These natives are punished, not by methods of frightfulness, but by economic pressure—the taking of their cattle. Then they submit. A little later—October 1875—Gordon discovers the Fola Falls and realises that the Nile will not allow her lakes to be reached by any toy steamer made by men.

"I fancied," he says, "that for some time I had heard a voice like thunder, which increased as we approached the river. At last we stood above it . . . and there it was, appalling to look at, far less to think of getting anything up or down, except in splinters. . . . It boiled down, twisting into all sorts of eddies, while the banks, steep and precipitous, presented a great length of view. These shoots last for two miles."

So there was nothing for it but to send for Gessi, now coming up from Khartoum, to organise hundreds of native carriers who would bear the steamer *Nyanza* in parts overland and launch her on Lake Albert. Gordon had already made up his mind that he would suppress what was evidently and indeed naturally an irresistible desire—to be the first surveyor of Lake Albert. Baker had discovered it, but it had not been explored. No! Gessi should accomplish this.

Meanwhile Gordon plunges away through jungle grass and desolate scrub-land to make a preliminary exploration of parts of the Victoria Nile. In the spring of 1876, Gessi returned, having surveyed Lake Albert and proclaimed it for the Khedive. By the summer of this year, Gordon had already mapped the whole 1,150-mile course of the Nile between Khartoum and Dufilé. He wished now to complete the survey of the stretch of the river connecting Lake Albert with Lake Victoria. Owing to the hostility of the King of Uganda he did not penetrate to Lake Victoria, but he came within sixty miles of it, to Niamyongo, one degree north of the Equator. The march to this point, and the return, constituted one of the most hazardous and daring exploits ever undertaken. You can still see Gordon advancing in torrential rain through terrible jungle, mapping as he goes. "I have never had such fatigue. It has utterly prostrated me —a deadly coldness and emptiness of the stomach makes you feel inclined to drop. Fifteen drops of chlorodine, however, set me up." The jungle is literally pathless, and at times the wild vines and convolvuli entangle and trip him up, so that he is terribly shaken by the falls. Mosquitoes in myriads and devastating heat! Natives with assegais crouching in ambush! Marshes and stinging hornets! And when Niamyongo has been reached, and the survey completed, there is the march back, partly along the river and partly across country to Lake Albert. One day the march was for miles down a narrow path with high grass on either side, the ominous drone of drum and horn advancing invisibly parallel with Gordon and his party. But they arrived back at Lake Albert in safety, and in October of 1876 Gordon determined to return to England. On Christmas Eve he was in London. "Looking back on the three years' vista, I have been much blessed in that long avenue," he wrote to his sister on the way home.[1]

He was only in England for little over a month. He had

[1] Dr. Allen's *Gordon and the Sudan*, P. Crabitès' *Gordon, the Sudan and Slavery*, Birckbeck Hill's *Gordon in Central Africa* and the *Letters to his Sister* have been my authorities for this part of the essay.

intended not to return to Africa, but the Khedive Ismail simply declined to contemplate his resignation. So Gordon arrived back in Cairo in February 1877. He was convinced that the slave-trade could only be effectively stopped if he had control of the whole Sudan, and he made his resumption of service conditional on his having the Sudan under his command. The Khedive at once agreed and united in one great Governor-Generalship the whole of the Sudan and Equatorial Provinces. The suppression of slavery and the improvement of communications were to be the main objectives.

For the next three years Gordon was supreme ruler of a dominion of a million square miles. Everywhere—from the capital Khartoum—stretched away, north, south, east and west, vast expanses of scorching desert. But in the west, if one rode some hundreds of miles, the desert gave place to green valleys, woods and mountains, and in the south to swamps, jungles and lakes. Writing to his sister in 1878, and recalling those earlier Equatorial days, Gordon becomes almost lyrical: "Take Lake Albert, a glorious amphitheatre of mountains with plenty of fine trees, picturesque little hamlets here and there, with grain and everything that men may need, flocks and cattle, and a splendid sheet of water stretching for miles, but a stillness that is dreadful. You feel yourself at the world's end." And of the desert, despite the terrible discomforts of endless camel rides in burning sun or blinding sandstorm, despite scorpions and swarming insects and eczema, he spoke with rapture: "The solitary grandeur of the desert makes one feel how vain

93

is the effort of man," and again: "The lights and shadows of this land are wonderful, the clearness of the air is so great." As for the camel, "it is a wonderful creature, and so comfortable with its silent cushion-like tread."

Of the Arab and negroid peoples inhabiting this vast area there were endless varieties of race and tribe, Nubian and Berberine, Bisharin and Baggara, and negroid Shilluk, Dinka and Nuer, to say nothing of Madi and Moogie. Gordon loved them all despite sudden outbursts of irritability: the Bedouin Arabs were "fine handsome fellows," the slave-raiders of Suleiman were like antelopes, and as for the blacks they were beautiful![1]

During these three years in the Sudan, Gordon consolidated the fame of his dynamic personal power. Hardly had he reached Khartoum and drawn up a scheme for the gradual abolition of slavery—a scheme which was the prelude to a convention signed a little later between Egypt and Great Britain—than he was called upon to suppress a dangerous rebellion in his westernmost province, Darfur. His first step was to relieve the beleaguered Egyptian garrisons with a force far smaller than those of the besieged. Fearful it was—he said himself—and fearful it must have been to see the Governor-General, arrayed in gold clothes, presented to him by the Khedive as a symbol of supreme authority, "flying along like a madman, with only a guide, as if he were pursued." Thus he relieved Fogia and thus

[1] ". . . But to lose all my beautiful black soldiers is enough to make one angry with those who have the direction of the future."—Gordon's Khartoum *Journals*, pp. 271-2, entry under November 2nd, 1884.

he relieved Dara. Then he moved on to El Fasher. But now Suleiman, son of the Arab soldier and slave-dealer Sebehr, a youthful warrior of twenty-two and a born commander of men, with four thousand slave-raiders had joined in the rebellion and was threatening the recently relieved Dara.

Like lightning, Gordon rushed back to Dara—outpacing his escort—and dumbfounded that garrison by the suddenness of his appearance. And next morning occurs the celebrated scene when he rode into Suleiman's camp of three thousand warriors with an escort of fifty horsemen. He orders Suleiman to attend him in Dara. Suleiman attends and is told that Gordon will break up his forces unless he submits. After three days of hesitation, Suleiman, already deserted by half his allies, sulkily returns to the slave-market of Shaka. Gordon follows him with four companions. Shaka had only once before been visited by a white man. The end of it is that Suleiman is ordered to retire to his province, and obeys. On his way back from Shaka, Gordon wrote:

"*Entre nous* I think I am conveying from Shaka to Obeid a caravan of slaves. I cannot help it. One man says that the seven women who are with him are his wives! I cannot disprove it. There are a number of children—the men say that they are their offspring! When you have got the ink which has soaked into blotting-paper out of it, then slavery will cease in these lands."

Apart from other evidences of the terrible vitality of

95

slavery—one could stop the caravans and strike off the chains, endeavour to suppress the central markets, break up gangs of raiders, but the snake was only scotched—Gordon was to find that Suleiman himself was incorrigible. A large part of the years 1878–9 is occupied with the campaign of Gessi, whom Gordon had again enlisted in his service, against the son of Sebehr. Later Gordon himself took the field in support of Gessi. The rebellion, after a dreadful toll of slaughter, for Suleiman's hosts fought like heroes, was suppressed. On July 15th, 1879, the youthful Suleiman was captured and shot by Gessi, acting under Gordon's instructions. Gordon had hardened his heart against the slave-traders; he had found suffering unspeakable. "Some of these poor slaves are mere skeletons. No female child, however young, passes unscathed by these scoundrels. . . . I declare, if I could stop this traffic, I would willingly be shot this night." With his intense belief that death was not an evil, he said he would shoot any number of slave-dealers without the least compunction if it would avail to stop the slave-trade.[1]

At last, worn out by his labours, Gordon resigned from the Khedive's service early in January 1880. His old friend and master, Ismail, had already been compelled to abdicate in the financial crisis of the preceding year. Gordon did not care for the new Khedive, Tewfik, the son of Ismail. He was depressed and over-wrought. But he retained his old humour. On January 8th, 1880, he wrote from Alexandria to his sister:

[1] See in particular *Letters to his Sister*, pp. 190–1.

" You will D.V. see me as soon as this letter, so I need not write what I have to say, for I will tell you in the kitchen where I can smoke."

Gordon spent little time in Augusta's kitchen. During the next four years he almost flew through the world, now in India in an incongruous and brief interlude as Private Secretary to the Viceroy, next in China preventing the Chinese from ruining themselves in a war with Russia, then Commandant of the island of Mauritius, afterwards in Basutoland on an abortive mission, finally in Palestine with a strange intensity following the feet in ancient times, and in Jerusalem itself building for himself a spiritual city.

"I wonder sometimes what is written in the roll of futurity for me," he wrote to his sister from Jerusalem in June 1883. "I scarcely think I am to dwell thus long, it is too quiet to last. . . . I believe more strongly than ever the pre-existence, and believe that the next world will be no new world to us. I think, if it were possible to have our hearts broken in the next world, broken they would be when we realise His love."[1]

Meanwhile, in Egypt and in the Sudan, which he vainly strove to put out of his thoughts just because his interest in them was so vital, a series of extraordinary events had occurred. In 1881 the religious rebellion of the Mahdi broke out in the Sudan. In that and the following year a revolutionary movement, half nationalist and half militarist, led by Arabi Pasha, got out of hand in Egypt. A number of

[1] *Letters to his Sister*, p. 322.

Europeans were massacred in Alexandria. England was compelled to intervene. The rebellious Egyptian Army was crushed by Wolseley. The British forces could not be withdrawn for fear of renewed anarchy. In the autumn of 1883 Sir Evelyn Baring was sent to Cairo as the British Consul-General. The Khedive and his Ministry continued to function, but the real ruler was Baring. In the Sudan the Mahdi's power had increased with enormous rapidity. Early in November an Egyptian army of ten thousand men under the command of Colonel Hicks was completely wiped out in a desert valley in Kordofan. When the tidings reached Cairo and London it was realised that a crisis of incredible difficulty had to be faced; namely, how the Egyptian garrisons in Khartoum, and other places less or more remote, were to be rescued.

As early as the autumn of 1882 the re-appointment of Gordon in the Sudan had been suggested to the Foreign Office by Lord Dufferin, who had been sent to Egypt on a special mission. But the Egyptian Government were unfavourable. As soon as news of the Hicks disaster was received in London, Lord Granville again took up the proposal. It was again rejected. Meanwhile, Gordon had decided to enter the service of the King of the Belgians with a view to suppressing the slave-trade in the Congo. How he arrived back in England on January 7th, 1884; how his name—already being discussed in *The Times* as High Commissioner for the Sudan[1]—was broadcast through

[1] On New Year's Day in a letter by Sir Samuel Baker; see Dr. Allen's definitive *Gordon and the Sudan*, p. 211.

England on January 9th, in an interview he gave to Stead, of the *Pall Mall Gazette*; how Lord Granville, backed by Mr. Gladstone, finally induced Sir Evelyn Baring to welcome Gordon for the purpose of helping in the evacuation of the Sudan; and how Gordon arrived in Cairo on January 24th— all this kaleidoscopic series of events we can merely record. Two days later, on January 26th, he set out on his mission to Khartoum. On that day he wrote to his sister:

"I feel quite happy, for I say, If God is with me, who can or will be hurtful to me? May He be glorified, the world and people of the Sudan be blessed, and may I be the dust under His feet."

On that very day, a year later, Khartoum was taken by the Mahdi, the city destroyed, and Gordon's body hacked in pieces.

"The dust under His feet"! We cannot doubt that Gordon foresaw, in sudden moments of almost Blake-like vision, some catastrophic and yet ordained event. Just before he left England, in parting from a friend, he said:

"Everyone has to fail, or we should have too high a belief in our own powers. As yet I have been successful: I have still to fail. I wish for humility, for God's guidance, and for resignation to God's will!"

The friend to whom Gordon spoke these words had talked to him about Newman's *Dream of Gerontius*, and he afterwards sent him that poem. The book reached Gordon in Khartoum on March 7th, just before the Dervishes had encircled the city. It was a curious gift, because the theme of the poem is the terror of death, and the agony of the last hours as they might be conceived by a saintly and yet naturally timid soul. It is difficult to think that the *Dream of Gerontius* can ever have had much meaning for Gordon. He had never been afraid of death. On the contrary, from his youth up he had courted it. What he dreaded above all things was failure, and the effect which failure might have on other people. This feeling was so strong that it caused a physical sensation, a pain in his heart to which he often refers in his letters and *Journals* when recounting any experience of extraordinary peril.

The word failure suggests not merely lack of success, but a lack of success arising out of avoidable mistakes. In this sense was Gordon's mission a failure, and, if so, was it his fault or the fault of the Gladstone Government? The true answer to this question I believe to be, that neither Gordon nor the Government failed, but that—as Mr. Gladstone himself expressed it in a letter written afterwards to Lord Hartington—the duties "were beyond human strength."[1] The more one reads of the lives and actions of those who were concerned in that fateful affair the more one experiences a feeling of the inevitable. Endless apologies or explanations have been written by the chief actors in the tragedy, and it is possible to see now, in the light of all the published facts, that this or that action was a mistake. But

[1] Morley's *Life of Gladstone*, Vol. III, pp. 196-7. And on February 23rd, 1885, Mr. Gladstone said: "The difficulties of the case have passed entirely beyond the limits of such political and military difficulties as I have known in the course of an experience of half a century."

all the facts and circumstances were not known to the different actors at the time as we know them to-day. Moreover, just because we know what they did not know, it is always easier to censure a Government than to criticise a heroic individual. As Lord Fitzmaurice says in his *Life of Lord Granville*:

" Neither did the memory of General Gordon perish in the horrors of the fall and sack of Khartoum. Therefore it is that, the man being of heroic stature, the Government through whose misfortune or fault he fell, will in this respect be one for which an impartial hearing will be difficult to obtain."[1]

Lord Cromer and Mr. Gladstone, looking back on events, took the view that it was a mistake ever to have sent Gordon, on account of the eccentricity of his character. But the plain fact is that the chance of evacuating the Sudan garrisons successfully was virtually a forlorn hope, and that Gordon was the one man who might have accomplished the impossible. When Lord Cromer was writing the weighty and sometimes enthralling chapters in his *Modern Egypt*, in which he alternates between praise and blame both of Gordon and of Gladstone, occasionally even of himself, he forgot that he fell completely under Gordon's sway at the beginning of the mission. "I am very glad he came," he wrote to Lord Granville, "for I believe he is the best man we could send."[2]

1 Lord Fitzmaurice's *Life of Lord Granville*, Vol. II, p. 400.
2 Lord Zetland's *Life of Lord Cromer*, p. 112. The letter is dated January 28th, 1884, just after Gordon's visit to Cairo *en route* for Khartoum.

Again, the Liberal Ministers, with the exception of Lord
Hartington, thought that Gordon had exceeded his instructions, that he was staying in Khartoum when he could
have got out, and that he was determined to "smash up the
Mahdi." When Gordon left England his mission was to
report on the situation, not to take executive action. But
the instructions left the Egyptian Government a free hand
to give him other duties, and, under Baring's advice, Gordon
was made Governor-General of the Sudan with the task of
actually effecting the evacuation. This change in the
instructions was fundamental in every way: Gordon regarded
them as his final marching orders; the Government at home,
though reluctantly acquiescing in the change at the time,
never got their original instructions out of their minds, nor
did they forget Gordon's own emphatic acceptance of them
in London. Again, in the subsequent criticism of the Liberal
Government, it is too often forgotten that they had become
involved in the affairs of Egypt against their will, that
they were determined not to involve themselves in the
Sudan, and that Russia took advantage of their entangle-
ments in 1884 to advance towards the Afghan frontier.
Subsequently, in the spring of 1885, we were within an ace
of war with Russia.[1]

Gordon's entry into Khartoum on February 18th was
triumphal, and the wavering tribes were overawed for a
short time. Then Gordon pressed his famous request for
Sebehr, the great Arab slave-raider and leader, to come up

[1] See, on the Russian complication, Lord Fitzmaurice's *Life of Lord
Granville*, Vol. II, ch. xii.

from Cairo, where he was a State prisoner, and take over the Governorship of the Sudan. Only thus could counter-force be rallied against the Mahdi, and an alternative Government be developed. That proposal, which Mr. Gladstone himself approved throughout and anti-slavery feeling in England condemned, was the only hope of successful evacuation. But Gordon never realised that it had been finally rejected, because the messages—the wires were cut on March 12th—never reached him.

The real truth was seen, as one might have expected, by Lord Hartington, who wrote to Lord Granville from Newmarket on September 14th, 1884, as follows:

". . . we have no proof that he (Gordon) could have done anything different from what he has done and is doing, or that he has wilfully disobeyed our instructions. We know that the despatch of the Egyptian employés, invalids, women, etc., from Khartoum was followed by the rising of the country between Khartoum and Berber, and by the attack on and fall of Berber. It is not possible that since those events he could have left Khartoum without sacrificing the lives of himself and those who followed him and also those whom he left behind. He had no alternative but to hold on at Khartoum and to keep the insurgents at bay. . . ."[1]

By this time the Government—Mr. Gladstone had been impressed by Lord Hartington's threat to resign—had decided to send a military expedition by the Nile route. For months the military authorities had been considering and differing over the alternative merits of the long Nile

[1] Lord Fitzmaurice's *Life of Lord Granville*, Vol. II, p. 397.

route and of the shorter Suakin–Berber route, and finally the Nile route won.[1] Whether the other route would have been better, who shall say? All we know is that the advance-guard of the Nile expedition arrived just two days after the fall of Khartoum.

No impartial person can deny that Gordon's estimate of the Mahdi's power and of the religious fervour behind the rebellion was altogether inadequate, nor that his messages were at times dreadfully confusing and misleading to plain men. "We were evidently," wrote Sir Charles Dilke, in February 1884, in his illuminating journals, "dealing with a wild man under the influence of that climate of Central Africa which acts even upon the sanest men like strong drink."[2] And, at the same time, no just person could say now that Gordon ought to have left the garrison and in-habitants whom he had come to save, merely in order to save himself.

In some of his flashes of vision he foresaw the future: he thought that Major Kitchener would make the best Governor-General of the Sudan, and he expressed his belief that "the Mahdi's business will be the end of slavery in the Sudan."[3] He did not foresee how these events would come about, nor that his own death would be the ultimate doorway through which hope would come to millions of the black people whom he loved.

[1] Morley's *Life of Gladstone*, Vol. III, pp. 164–5. See also Allen's *Gordon and the Sudan*, p. 348; also pp. 374–5.

[2] *Life of Sir Charles Dilke*, by Miss G. Tuckwell, Vol. II, p. 41.

[3] Gordon's *Journals at Khartoum*, pp. 362–3, and p. 386.

Let us, therefore, not wait to see those Dervishes creeping stealthily past the lines between the river and the ramparts at dawn of January 26th, 1885, nor listen to the shrieks and cries, nor watch the wild rush up the palace stairs, the hurrying feet, the spear-thrusts and the garments rolled in blood. All that is ended.

> *His servants He, with new acquist*
> *Of true experience from this great event,*
> *With peace and consolation hath dismissed,*
> *And calm of mind, all passion spent.*

Chapter Three

DIARISTS OF THE EIGHTEENTH CENTURY[1]

In George Saintsbury's *A Short History of English Literature* an honourable place is assigned to two diarists of the seventeenth century; one is Samuel Pepys, and the other is John Evelyn. No one will accuse Mr. Saintsbury of lack of catholicity in criticism; he was, and is, the most catholic of all the critics and the most fair-minded. Moreover he is, I venture to think, on the whole the most illuminating, having regard to the great span which he covered and the vast range of his reading and scholarship.

Nevertheless it is surprising to find that no diarist, as such, of the eighteenth century finds a place in his *Short History*, unless one includes Swift and his *Journal to Stella* at the beginning of the century. I think it is permissible to include Swift among the company of diarists, if one interprets that title in a broad sense, just as the early pages of Dorothy Wordsworth's *Journal* entitle Dorothy to a supreme place at the end of the century. It is, of course, the case that the variety and extent of diary writing in the eighteenth century have only recently come to be realised, partly owing to the three admirable volumes of critical anthologies—

[1] This essay was written as a paper for the English Society of Girton College, Cambridge, and was read on November 22nd, 1935.

English Diaries, More English Diaries and *Scottish and Irish Diaries*—produced by Lord Ponsonby, and partly owing to the discovery of unknown manuscripts. It is typical of Mr. Saintsbury's catholicity that he should at once have welcomed[1] Lord Ponsonby's pioneering work, just as he immediately recognised the place of Parson Woodforde.[2] But I am still surprised that John Wesley's *Journals* were not deemed worthy of Mr. Saintsbury's notice. For Wesley's *Journals* are perhaps the most important among the diaries of the eighteenth century and—though so utterly different—I am inclined to think that Wesley's name should stand next to Pepys in the hierarchy of diarists.

In the magnificent city of literature with its many mansions we cannot afford to ignore any part of the plan. Pre-eminent, of course, are the noble thoroughfares, "the cloud-capped towers, the gorgeous palaces." But turn down any of the numberless side streets and how pleasant, how exciting they are!

Pepys, of course, resides in one of the most curiously architected and yet one of the most charming houses in a principal thoroughfare. He stands head and shoulders above all the diarists. Wesley, I myself believe, occupies that pleasant Georgian mansion on the corner of a lesser street leading directly into a thoroughfare. Parson Woodforde will be found—but this may be piety or prejudice or just stark insensibility on my part—in that neat Rectory whose

[1] In *A Second Scrap Book.*

[2] Not only in the columns of *The Times* but in a number of letters to me.

garden wall at the back, by a side door, communicates with
Pepys's orchard.

In this essay I propose to gossip first—but with becoming
brevity—about the few diaries of the eighteenth century
which have always been regarded as literature in the elect
sense of that term, next about a number of diaries which
at least must be accorded some place in the realm of letters,
and finally about Wesley and Woodforde, whose place some
critics would put high, and some perhaps would put low.
I do not propose to tear any passion to tatters, nor to tie
myself up in the knots of consistent principle—partly
because there are few dogs so dull as your consistent dog,
and partly because gossip, after all, has its privileges.

There is one general characteristic of all diaries or journals
worthy of the name; and here I must observe parenthetically
that there is no distinction to be drawn between a journal
and a diary, both words mean the same thing in the dictionary. The general characteristic is that if they are worth
anything at all they very quickly introduce the reader
intimately to the writer, as intimately, that is to say, as one
can ever hope in this world to be introduced to any other
fellow being.

Take Swift's *Journal to Stella*. The fact, by the way, that it
is in the form of letters sent at intervals of ten days or a
fortnight does not prevent it from being a diary or journal,
for it was written up every day of the intervals in the true
manner of the diarist. The great man stalks into your room
at once, and, for that matter, half the brilliant figures of
that glistering period 1710–13. On October 30th, 1712:

"the Duke of Hamilton gave me a pound of snuff today, admirable good. I wish DD had it, and Ppt too,[1] if she likes it. It cost me a quarter of an hour of his politics, which I was forced to hear. Lady Orkney is making me a writing-table of her own contrivance, and a bed nightgown. She is perfectly kind, like a mother. . . . The other day we had a long discourse with her about love; and she told us a saying of her sister Fitzharding, which I thought excellent, that 'in men, desire begets love, and in women love begets desire'!"

And did you know that that most expressive description of the female sex—or some of them—as being "Sauce-boxes" was as old as Queen Anne—Stella and her friend are called "Sauce-boxes" by Swift as a term of endearment, or that you could smell new-mown hay in the meadows of London in 1711, or that the mere thought of cherry trees in Ireland could move Swift suddenly to write a simple line of prose as lyrical as poetry: "the cherry trees, by the river side, my heart is set upon." And yet he could not tear himself away from London and the Court! Or was it, not the Lord Treasurer and the wits and the intellectual life that kept him there longer than he had intended, but Vanessa?

The next diary of outstanding literary merit is Fielding's *Journal of a Voyage to Lisbon*. In this serene and touching work, written in the last year, 1754, and even in the last months, of his life, when he knew perfectly well that so soon he would be silent, we meet the author of *Tom Jones* face to face. Neither in letters nor in autobiography nor in poetry

[1] His pet names for Mrs. Dingley and Stella.

would it have been possible to become more closely acquainted with a great man, or, at least, with this great man.
The diary form suited him. He could thereby unburden
himself of this "too, too solid flesh," and he could describe
with his incomparable vitality the actors and the action of
the passing hour. He was too weak to walk and had to be
carried everywhere, to be literally hoisted hither and thither.
His countenance was so emaciated and so signed with the
seal of death that women and children shrank from him as
he passed. But that final power of the spirit over matter,
which is a perpetual miracle, enables him to persuade us
that grief would be out of place. How can we remember
sad things for more than a moment when the comedy of
life is so vividly portrayed—the superstitious and stout-
hearted captain of the ship, the brutal and splendid sailors,
the odious lodging-house mistress at Ryde, the kitten who
fell overboard and the surgeons who so egregiously failed
to relieve Mrs. Fielding's devastating attack of tooth-ache?
And then, suddenly, in a vivid aside we see the British fleet
at sea as our ancestors saw it and we can never see it again—
in the full panoply of glorious sail and oaken wall. "A fleet
of ships," says Fielding, "is, in my opinion, the noblest
object which the art of man hath ever produced: and far
beyond the power of those architects who deal in brick,
in stone, or in marble." In 1782 Cobbett saw the same
spectacle and describes in his autobiography the memorable
effect of it on his mind. This is one of the rewards of diary
reading. In the twinkling of an eye we see things as they
once were.

The next literary giant of the eighteenth century who can be numbered among the diarists is Gibbon. We first hear of his journal in that famous *Autobiography* of his which one can never tire of reading and re-reading. But there the selected passages are a little heightened, touched up and manipulated, not only by Gibbon himself, but by his editor, Lord Sheffield. It was only six years ago that the first complete text of the journal was published under the editorship of Mr. D. M. Low. The day-to-day, or nearly day-to-day, record only covers a very short period—from the summer of 1760 to January 1763. But it is good to have it. It introduces us in a very pleasant way to a person who can never seem otherwise than portentous on account of the overwhelming weight of his scholarship. Gibbon is in the Militia and either living at Beriton or marching about in Wiltshire or Dorset or Hampshire, reading Homer and Strabo and Quintilian and French literature and at the same time leading a humdrum military life, and meeting ordinary men and women of the country squire type. His ironic comments are of the best vintage in that kind. "The house [Lord Shaftesbury's] appears excessively large, but very irregular. We did not see the inside. His Lordship came out to ask us in, but the invitation was so faint that we declined it." There is an excellent description of Bryanston, now a well-known public school, and of its owner, Mr. Portman: "It is only to be feared that his love of fox-hunting, hatred to London, and constant court of dependant persons, may in time reduce him to the contemptible character of a meer country squire." Or take this of Sir

Thomas Worsley, remembering that he is his commanding officer, Lieut.-Colonel of the South Hampshire Militia, Gibbon being but a captain in that corps.

"May 28, 1762 was spent very disagreeably. Sir Thomas is determined to go to Spa, and only came to settle things before his departure. So that I was entertained the whole day with a long detail of sensible schemes he will never execute and schemes he will execute which are highly ridiculous."

Or consider Mr. Edmund Pleydwell of Millbourne:

" He is a very good natured Country gentleman, affable to everybody, indifferent as to his company, and ready to do whatever they please. In a word, a most excellent candidate for a County. His wife is a little ill-natured thing that seems to torment him continually."

A diarist of tantalisingly brief compass is the poet Gray. For a fortnight in October 1769, Gray made a tour of the Lake District and during that time kept a journal. It is typical of Gray that his journal should be so short. After all, the whole of his poetry can be gathered together within the compass of one hundred and fifty well-printed pages. Only his wonderful letters, now so recently re-edited and collected, run into three stout volumes. Here is a passage from his journal:

"In the evening walked alone down to the Lake by the side of Crow-Park after sunset and saw the solemn colouring of night draw on, the last gleam of sunshine fading away

on the hill-tops, the deep serene of the waters, and the long
shadows of the mountains thrown across them, till they
nearly touched the hithermost shore. At distance heard the
murmur of many waterfalls not audible in the day-time.
Wished for the moon, but she was 'dark to me and silent,
hid in her vacant interlunar cave.' "

After the tour of the Lakes, Gray returned, in due course,
"gently" as he himself expresses it, to his beloved Cambridge. I can never walk between Pembroke and Peterhouse
—Gray's spiritual homes—without a feeling that somewhere
near me is the author of the *Elegy*; he looks at the passing
throng—how shocked he would have been to see Cambridge
invaded by the other sex—with a rather austere countenance
which is merely a mask to conceal a heart trembling with
powerful emotions, a passionate love of truth, of beauty and,
above all, of the passing generations who in their golden
time adorn and are adorned by the University.

The last two literary figures of the eighteenth century who
fall within the diary net are women—Fanny Burney and
Dorothy Wordsworth. The authoress of *Evelina* was an
inveterate diarist, and her facile pen has filled eight stout
volumes with diaries and letters which begin in 1768,
and continue in a constant stream till well into the nineteenth century. She is a master-hand at reproducing conversation, and, if you wish to hear with your own ears George
III's opinion of Shakespeare—"Sad stuff? What? What?"—
you must refer to Miss Burney. She certainly can be exceedingly amusing. At a dinner party in Grosvenor Square in, I
think, March 1781, at which were present both Boswell

and Dr. Johnson, and Fanny and her father, and a Mr. B.,

"Mr. B. was just as absurdly pompous as at Brighton; and in the midst of dinner, without any sort of introduction, or reason, or motive, he called out aloud: 'Sweet are the slumbers of the charming maid!' A laugh from all parties, as you may imagine, followed this exclamation; and he bore it with amazing insensibility."

It was fortunate for Mr. B. that Dr. Johnson did not hear this irrelevant remark, otherwise, we may be certain that his fate would have been that of a mouse which had carelessly run under a steam-roller.

Of Dorothy Wordsworth little need be said, partly because her *Journals* are so well known, and partly because the eighteenth century can only claim those written in 1798. Still, if one wants to understand the place, and atmosphere of dream-like beauty in which the *Lyrical Ballads* were composed by her brother and by Coleridge, it is necessary to read the Alfoxden *Journals*: February 3rd, 1798:

"A mild morning, the windows open at breakfast, the redbreasts singing in the garden. Walked with Coleridge over the hills. The sea at first obscured by vapour; that vapour afterwards slid in one mighty mass along the sea-shore. . . . I never saw such a union of earth, sky, and sea. . . . Gathered sticks in the wood; a perfect stillness. The redbreasts sang upon the leafless boughs."

It was in that same month of February 1798, you will remember, that Coleridge wrote his lovely *Frost at Midnight*, which contains the lines:

Storm and Peace

Therefore all seasons shall be sweet to thee,
Whether the summer clothe the general earth
With greenness, or the redbreast sit and sing
Betwixt the tufts of snow on the bare branch
Of mossy apple-tree. . . .

Reluctantly we leave the company of Swift, Fielding, Gibbon, Gray, Fanny Burney and Dorothy Wordsworth. And yet I am not sure that the company we are about to enter is really less delightful. Only it is very different, and as the list of names is considerably longer it will only be possible to establish a mere nodding acquaintance with a few of them. You may, at your leisure, wish to meet people like the Earl of Egmont, Dr. Rutty (who coined such a phrase as "a frappish cholerick day"), Mrs. Browne, Thomas Turner (who is capable of such an entry as "My old, I wish I could say my worthy, friend, Mr. Tucker of Lewis came to dine with me"), the Rev. William Jones, Thomas Hollis, Windham the Statesman, and a number of others whom Lord Ponsonby deals with in his admirable volumes. For the moment we must content ourselves with an introduction to four diarists not represented in the Ponsonby volumes— Thomas Hearne, the Oxford antiquary, the Rev. William Cole, the Cambridge antiquary, Viscount Torrington, the rural rider of the 1780's and 90's, and the Rev. Charles Wesley—brother of the great diarist of the century.

Thomas Hearne, born in 1678, son of a poor parish clerk, would never have been able to reach Oxford and Edmund Hall there, but for the generosity of a patron, Mr. Francis Cherry. Mr. Cherry did well for scholarship, for Hearne's passion for the past, and specially for his country's past, produced volume after volume of the raw material of history in the shape *inter alia* of editions of the English Chroniclers, who had never before been accessible. His industry was enormous. The *Dictionary of National Biography* gives the titles of thirty-seven learned works which he sponsored or edited. And in addition to all this he jotted down from day to day all sorts of curious observations, notes, quotations, comments and gossip, beginning in 1705 and continuing till almost the day of his death thirty years later. He disliked the word diary, and his various comments on mortality are called Hearne's *Collections*, publication of which has at last been completed by the Oxford Historical Society in eleven volumes. But diaries they really are. Pope attacked him in the third book of the *Dunciad*[1] as Wormius:

> *But who is he, in closet close y-pent,*
> *Of sober face, with learned dust besprent?*
> *Right well mine eyes arede the myster wight,*
> *On parchment scraps y-fed, and Wormius hight.*
> *To future ages may thy dulness last,*
> *As thou preserv'st the dulness of the past!*

While Pope was indulging in this odious form of publicity, quiet antiquary Hearne was noting down in his MS. diary, under date July 18th, 1729:

"Mr. Alexander Pope, the Poet's Father, was a poor ignorant man, a tanner at Binfield in Berks. . . . This Alexander Pope, tho he be an English Poet, yet he is but

1 Lines 185–90.

an indifferent scholar, mean at Latin and can hardly read Greek. He is a very ill-natured man, and covetous and excessively proud."

It is impossible not to like Hearne: the oddity of his entries endears him at once. Among his notes for February 10th, 1731, is the following:

"About three weeks since died Mary Pulcher at Little-more by Oxford. She was a strangely merry, laughing Woman. She was never married. She was 75 years old. She was found dead, stark naked, in the lowest room of the House (her brother's house) with whom she lived, tho till of late she had generally lived at Oxford. 'Tis supposed she was seized suddenly (for she went to bed well), and tumbled down stairs."

And who would not wish to meet Mistress Hester Luffe of Oxford, who died, alas, on February 26th, 1709, though Hearne's note about her does not appear till April 1st, 1730:

"She was a most charming sweet creature, and admired by all who saw her, and 'tis a pity she had not a Fortune equal to her Beauty. A very fine beautifull young Nobleman of Xt Church addressed himself to her, being perfectly in Love with her, and very frequently in her Company, and 'twas said there was a Contract, but he fell off, perhaps by the contrivance of his friends, and went a travelling, wch so affected her (for she doated upon him) that she soon decayed and languished away. When she lived with her Father in St Peter's in the East (the house where they lived being afterwards from thence, & is to this day, stiled Luffe Hall) St Peter's Church used to be thronged with young gentlemen, when she was there. One day, when she was coming from the said Church, it being a very slippery season, in Queen's Coll. Lane she happened to fall down, and her coats flying up, discovered what pleased the young gentlemen, who used to be very merry upon it, but much abashed the young Lady, who had always the Character of a very modest Virtuous person. I remember once a Gentleman of Wealth and Fortune, and of a good character in other respects, told the company where I happened to be, that on that day he came down Heddington Hill, he met Mrs Hester Luffe, and that he had a full view of her, and believed her to be the prettiest Woman and most complete Beauty (of wch he was a great Judge, being very amorous) that ever he saw in his life."

Hearne was not always as charitable as this. He could be extremely caustic, as for instance on the Rev. Charles Dingley, lately Fellow of Corpus Xti College, whose "continual bibbing of brandy and other strong liquors . . . quite drowned his parts and understanding, if ever he had any."

Hearne lived all his life in Oxford, was a devoted Jacobite and non-juror, and would have succeeded to the Librarianship of the Bodleian if he had been conscientiously able to take the oaths of loyalty to the Hanoverian dynasty. But this he could not bring himself to do.

We pass to the Rev. William Cole, the friend of Walpole and Gray, the distinguished Cambridge antiquary whose diaries are now coming out—two volumes have appeared so far—under the editorship of Mr. F. G. Stokes and general introduction of Miss Helen Waddell. Like Hearne, Cole can be uncommonly caustic in his comments on mankind; but his disposition, we fancy, was distinctly more irritable than Hearne's. On the other hand, for a number of years he had parochial duties to worry him, and had not the same entire leisure to devote to beloved antiquarian studies. Altogether a very pleasant person and parson! Here he is talking angrily to himself about a neighbouring farmer:

"But Hogs are the proper Combatants with Hogs. I own the Man's Brutality quite frightens me."

Or a neighbouring parson annoys him and he lets himself go as follows:

"Last year we were stunned with his Scraps from Plato: But being so full of my Lord Temple and my Lord Verney, whom he has much visited this year, he is generally so full of them, that his erudition is the more neglected."

The pleasant side of Cole's character emerges chiefly when he speaks of his servants, especially, "My Tom," or of his parochial services and charities, or of his cherished books. His style is curiously contorted if he embarks on any lengthy account of things. On the other hand, he had the art of sketching in a vivid portrait in a few lines—as for instance of this out-of-door, breezy couple:

"the most suitable Match that ever was made in Point of Tempers, they equally living on Horseback, in the Fields,

120

by the Side of Rivers, or any where but in their House, which is at Mursley, where their Father has established them in a Farm, after failing at Baldock in a Malting."

These extracts are from his *Blecheley Diary, 1765–1767.* Cole was Rector of Bletchley, in Buckinghamshire, from 1753 to 1767. From 1767 to the day of his death, 1782, he lived first at Waterbeach and then at Milton, so as to be near Cambridge, which was his spiritual home. His antiquarian researches into the parochial antiquities of Cambridgeshire, into the history of King's (his College), of the University, of Ely and into genealogical, topographical and other matters, fill a hundred or so folio volumes of manuscripts which, with excellent sense, he deposited in the British Museum. Like all good antiquaries he was immensely generous with his help to other scholars, and since his death his manuscript collections in the British Museum have been a quarry for students.

The diaries of Lieut.-Colonel John Byng, afterwards the fifth Viscount Torrington, have only very recently been published under the editorship of Mr. C. B. Andrews. Two volumes have appeared, and the third and last volume is on the way. They contain day-to-day descriptions of his tours through England and Wales between 1781 and 1794. They are pleasant reading, and give good descriptions of the countryside at a time when the Industrial Revolution was beginning to change the landscape. He was well read. Not many officers in the Brigade of Guards, we apprehend, nor for that matter many persons commonly supposed to be educated, are as familiar as Byng was with Shakespeare, Milton and Cervantes, as well as with the great literary figures of his own century. Utterly unlike Cobbett in outlook, character and style, he nevertheless resembles Cobbett in his passionate love of the countryside. He belonged to that pioneering company—Walpole and Gray were the most distinguished members of it—who were discovering that the Middle Ages were not barbaric, and that Gothic architecture was one of the supreme manifestations of human genius. "How superior to a lumbering Grecian St. Paul's is Lincoln Cathedral"—he feels in 1791. And then suddenly you come across one of those startling observations which are the treasure trove of the reader of diaries. He is speaking of that remarkable revolution which makes the second half of the eighteenth century differ from all the centuries which preceded it—the opening up of the country by the making and remaking of roads, and the digging of canals. For the first time since the Roman occupation of Britain there was effective communication between the different parts of the island. For his part, Byng, writing in June 1791, conceives:

"If my Journals should remain legible, or be perused at the end of 200 years, there will, even then, be little curious in them relative to travell, or the people; Because our Island is now so Explored; Our Roads in general are so fine; and our speed has reached the Summit."

Byng's idea of supreme speed was perhaps a spurt of fifteen miles an hour, in one of the fastest mail coaches. No! we can only hope that this wistful rider through rural

England no longer haunts the King's highway, nor endeavours to trot down one of the great trunk roads on his faithful nag.

Apart from the fact that they were both clergymen of the Church of England, there is nothing in common between the Rev. William Cole and the Rev. Charles Wesley, the next clerical diarist whom we are to consider. Charles Wesley was the younger brother of the supreme founder and leader of the Methodist movement, but there was only a difference of four years in their age: both were born in the early part of Queen Anne's reign, and both lived to over fourscore years, Charles till 1788, John till 1791. Charles is chiefly known as a hymn writer. "Of Charles Wesley's 6,500 hymns," says Lord Ernle, in his now classical *The Psalms in Human Life*, "some are unsurpassed in beauty, and rank among the finest in the English language."

How familiar are some of Charles's hymns! "Christ whose glory fills the skies," "Jesu, Lover of my soul," "Let saints on earth in concert sing," "Soldiers of Christ arise," "Lo! He comes with clouds descending," "Hark! the herald-angels sing," these are but six out of the thirty which will be found in *Hymns Ancient and Modern*. And then there is that prayer, written as a hymn, familiar for over a century to millions of children at their mother's knee—"Gentle Jesu, meek and mild."

It is curious that Charles Wesley's *Journal* should be so little known. Extracts from it were originally published in biographies of him, but it was not until 1849 that the main text of such parts of it as had survived were published

123

under the excellent editorship of Thomas Jackson. I do
not think there has been any later edition, though the first
three years were edited in greater detail by the Rev. John
Telford in 1909. Parts of the *Journal*, specially those for
the earlier years, are of deep human and historical interest.
The *Journal* begins in the year 1736, when Charles and John
Wesley were missionising in the just-founded colony of
Georgia—Charles, in fact, acting as secretary to General
Oglethorpe, the noble philanthropist who was himself
the founder of the settlement. It continues till 1756,
but with considerable gaps, particularly during the later
years.

His descriptions of the great but eccentric Oglethorpe,
of the gentlemanly rogue, Appee, of the hardships of
colonial life, of a drunken sea-captain, of his evangelical
labours and travels in this country, as his brother's right-
hand helper, are of literary merit, quite apart from their
specific interest. Here is a description of a storm, in the
entry of October 28th, 1736, and parenthetically let it
be observed that it is in diaries and autobiographies that
we realise most vividly the ghastly experiences of our sea-
faring ancestors in the days of small sailing ships. I can
give here only a short passage from the entry:

"It was now about three in the afternoon, and the storm
at the height. I endeavoured to encourage poor Mr Brig and
Cutler, who were in the utmost agony of fear. I prayed with
them, and for them, till four; at which time the ship
made so much water, that the Captain, finding it otherwise
impossible to save her from sinking, cut down the mizen

mast. In this dreadful moment, I bless God, I found the comfort of hope; and such joy in finding I could hope, as the world can neither give nor take away. I had that conviction of the power of God, present with me, overruling my strongest passion, fear, and raising me above what I am by nature, as surpassed all rational evidence, and gave me a taste of the divine goodness."

The story of the storm ends thus:

"The wind was still as high as ever, but the motion rather less violent since the cutting of the mast, and we did not ship quite so much water. I laid me down utterly exhausted; but my distemper was so increased, it would not suffer me to rest. Toward morning the sea heard and obeyed the divine voice, 'Peace, be still.'"

It is impossible here to give any idea of Charles Wesley's experiences as an itinerant preacher, but there is a humorous quotation, under date October 25th, 1743, which I cannot forbear, of an unfortunate witness, who was accusing John Wesley before a local Justice: "To be plain, Sir, if I must speak the truth, all the fault I find with him is, that he preaches better than our Parsons." For the most part, however, the *Journal* is profoundly serious. Indefatigably moving about England and Wales, riding on one occasion 300 miles in five days, he was ceaselessly conscious of his calling. Doubtless it was with a vivid memory of many a lonely journey that he wrote the exquisite hymn, which must rank high in the rare realm of religious poetry:

Come, O Thou Traveller unknown,
 Whom still I hold, but cannot see!
My company before is gone,
 And I am left alone with Thee;
With Thee all night I mean to stay,
And wrestle till the break of day.

At this point it may be well to pause for a moment, and to consider why men and women of very different characters, abilities and situations in the world have kept diaries. No doubt there are several answers and explanations, some simple and some complicated. For the moment I will only suggest one which, I fancy, may cover in whole or in part at least a considerable proportion of cases. Diary writing is the literary medium of talking to oneself. The Rev. William Cole, quoting someone else, describes it as "The Importance of a Man to his own Self." That is, perhaps, a better way of putting it. Virginia Woolf, discussing Parson Woodforde in *The Common Reader* (Second Series) illustrates the point in her own delightful way, at the same time carrying it a step further: "When James Woodforde opened one of his neat manuscript books he entered into conversation with a second James Woodforde, who was not quite the same as the reverend gentleman who visited the poor and preached in the church." How difficult it is to know oneself! Perhaps, if one tries to talk, to write to oneself, the mystery will become a little clearer. And then—like turning over an old volume of snapshots over a period of years—one will notice the changes and the fixities of one's character. It is not, I think, essential that the diary writer, in order to achieve excellence in his art, should only write to or for himself. It is true that certain diaries were written—as far as can be ascertained—with no intention whatever of publication. Pepys is a case in point. So is Parson Woodforde. On the other hand Fielding's *Journal* was written deliberately with the object of publication, and Wesley's *Journal* was, in considerable part, published by himself in his own lifetime. But though Fielding and Wesley wrote with an eye on the public—not in the least seeking applause, but merely with the object of putting certain things on record— that is not to say that they were not also at the time of writing, talking to themselves. For it is pretty plain that they were.

And I should not like to assert that Pepys and Woodforde *never*—in their secret souls—contemplated their diaries being read by anyone else at all. I doubt if they ever would have admitted any such thought even to themselves, and perhaps it would have shocked them deeply if the idea had consciously emerged in their minds. Nevertheless, the fact remains that neither Pepys nor Woodforde ever took the quite simple precaution either of burning their diaries or of giving explicit directions that they should be destroyed after their death. Such action, they may subconsciously have reflected, would be rather like suicide, like smashing the mirror you hold in your hand. Again, they believed that the body in which they would be raised would be very different from this earthly body, and what would it matter what the world thought of them meanwhile, when so profound a change would make all such ideas and reflections altogether irrelevant and unimportant, indeed would make all past things as though they had never been?

One further general question may be asked: what qualities are needed for excellence in the art of diary writing? My own answer would be this—a peculiar interest in life itself, a sense of proportion, an innate understanding of the importance of little things in the make-up of life, a deep sense of truth and the power to convey its impression in compendious phrase.

But time passes, and we must hasten to meet the last two diarists whom we propose to consider in this many-sided eighteenth century—John Wesley and Parson Woodforde.

The more one studies the life of John Wesley the more it becomes clear that he was one of the great figures of history. Suddenly there appears, in that world of relative tranquillity, of growing wealth, of social comfort—specially for the privileged classes, of classical calm and culture, of philosophic and worldly religion, of disciplined and sometimes disdainful intellectualism, a small figure of dynamic force who not only transformed the moral outlook of his time, but lighted a torch in this country and America by which millions of men have been guided and enabled to guide their fellow men. Here is a clergyman of the Church of England who to the day of his death protested his fidelity to that calm fold, a classical scholar and Fellow of Lincoln College, Oxford, a Tory in politics, a man in many respects very much of his time, who, nevertheless, is a man of all time. How does this come about? To say that he was a born administrator and ruler of men—Macaulay says that he was not inferior to Richelieu in the art of government[1]—is only to give a partial explanation. The real truth is that the light which lights every man who comes into the world shone in him with the strength and brightness of a star "in lone splendour, hung aloft the night."

The *Journal* which he kept for fifty-five years—sixty-six if one includes the shorter entries in what he called his diary, to distinguish it from the fuller entries of the *Journal*—explains the source and constant inspiration of this light, and at the same time gives a picture, unsurpassed in range and variety, of the moral and material background of his time. Moreover, if it be a principal function of literature to move, not only the mind and the imagination, but the emotions, then I would claim that Wesley's *Journal*, time and again, achieves greatness in the literary sense. Professor Oliver Elton, in his comprehensive and admirable *Survey of English Literature, 1730–1780*,[2] says of Wesley, "he can be a very good and something like a great writer." Well! I would put it higher than that.

The standard edition of Wesley's *Journal* extends to eight capacious volumes, and even the shorter—though nearly complete—edition in Everyman's Library runs to four volumes of some 500 pages each. It will, therefore, be impossible to illustrate the reasons why I place Wesley's

1 And Macaulay's great-nephew, Mr. George Trevelyan, describes him as "one of the greatest missionaries and the greatest religious organisers of all history" (*History of England*, p. 519).

2 Vol. II, p. 213.

Journal as high as I do: it is only possible to give an idea or two of its significance.

It was on May 24th, 1738—after a period of spiritual numbness—that there came to John Wesley what seemed to him the outstanding experience of his life. On that day, at five o'clock in the morning, he opened his Greek Testament in the Second Epistle of St. Peter and his eye fell upon these words: "There are given unto us great and precious promises, even that ye should be partakers of the divine nature." In the afternoon he went to St. Paul's Cathedral and heard the anthem "Out of the deep have I called unto thee, O Lord: Lord, hear my voice." In the evening, while he was listening to Luther's preface to the Epistle to the Romans, there came to him that sense of a living faith in Christ which, despite his good works and Christian way of life from early youth, he felt he had hitherto lacked. This living faith henceforth remained with him to his dying day. It carried him through extraordinary experiences of danger to life and limb, through menace and mockery, through ceaseless journeyings by land and water. Henceforth till the age of eighty-eight he preached the Gospel through the length and breadth of the United Kingdom, never relaxing his labours, rising at four in the morning, and covering, until old age, mainly on horseback, some 4,500 miles every year. This is the sort of thing that happened in the earlier years of his mission, and before he had accomplished that miraculous transformation of the wild eighteenth-century mobs who haunted the background of men's dreams. It was October 20th, 1743, and he was at Wednesbury in Staffordshire:

"To attempt speaking was in vain; for the noise on every side was like the roaring of the sea; so they dragged me along till we came to the town, where seeing the door of a large house open, I attempted to go in; but a man, catching me by the hair, pulled me back into the middle of the mob. They made no more stop till they had carried me through the main street, from one end of the town to the other. I continued speaking all the time to those within hearing, feeling no pain or weariness."

Finally the leader of the mob succumbed to Wesley's dynamic power, and was the means of his rescue. Wesley adds that throughout he felt the same presence of mind as though "I had been sitting in my own study." Once it crossed his mind that, if he were thrown into the river,

"it would spoil the papers that were in my pocket. For myself I did not doubt but I should swim across, having but a thin coat and a light pair of boots."

Here is a very different scene towards the end of his life: he is in Ireland at Tandragee, on June 11th, 1789:

"Such a congregation I have not seen since I came into the kingdom; neither such a pleasing place, shaded with tall, spreading trees, near which ran a clear river: and all the people listened with quiet and deep attention, to, 'Drink of the Water of Life freely.' "

Finally there is the entry on January 1st, 1790, when he was eighty-seven—he died in March of the following year:

"I am now an old man, decayed from head to foot. My eyes are dim; my right hand shakes much; my mouth is hot and dry every morning. I have a lingering fever almost every day. My motion is weak and slow. However, blessed be God, I do not slack my labour. I can preach and write still."

So we take our leave of Wesley, turn down a pleasant lane in Norfolk and find ourselves in the parsonage of another clergyman of that Church of England which gathers within its magnanimous, mild and comprehensive fold so many good men, and so many good minds.

As I have already written five introductions to the five-volume edition of Parson Woodforde's *Diary*, and have now written a sixth for the single-volume edition which has just been published by the Oxford University Press, I find it not easy to say anything very new or very original about my beloved parson.

But this much can at once be said. It would be hard to find any two men who differed more in mind, character and outlook than John Wesley and James Woodforde. Indeed the only thing they had in common was their belief in God, and their devotion to the Church of England. Only two years before his death Wesley had written a trenchant letter to a cantankerous disciple, who was highly critical of the Church: "To renounce going to Church," Wesley rapped out, "is, in fact, to renounce connection with me."[1] Parson Woodforde's conception of the Church's mission and duty differed pretty profoundly from Wesley's. During the last years of his life, indeed, he delegated his clerical duties to a

[1] Wesley's *Letters*, edited by John Telford, Vol. VIII, pp. 177–9: letter dated October 25th, 1879.

curate, having, it must be surmised, undermined his
health—he was only sixty-three when he died—by an
excessive devotion to dinner and a blissful eighteenth-
century belief in the efficacy of port wine.

As an undergraduate at Oxford, Fellow and subsequently
Sub-Warden of New College, to say nothing of Pro-
Proctor of the University, his steady addiction to port must
have made him a close rival of that great Cambridge man
and Prime Minister whom he so much admired, the
younger Pitt. We must not, however, exaggerate the port
motif in Parson Woodforde's life: certainly since his
earlier Oxford days when he had a painful experience of
falling on the back of his head, he never took so much as
to become, as he so expressively describes it, "disguised."
The truth is that wine and beer of the best, roast beef,
pig's face, rabbits smothered with onions, turkey, goose,
partridges, swan roasted with currant jelly sauce, haunch
of venison, and, dear me, a vast variety of puddings and
sweets covering pages of index, are generous things, and
Parson Woodforde had a generous disposition. That is all
there is to say about it. If you want to know what eighteenth-
century hospitality really was, just call in on the Reverend
James Woodforde and his beloved niece Nancy, stay a day
or two at Weston Parsonage in Norfolk, and, in the interest
of health, don't forget to join with them in taking a good
dose of rhubarb before you go to bed!

In first singling out this food and drink aspect of Parson
Woodforde's life I am merely making a concession to a
popular conception of the interest of his *Diary*. That aspect,

however, is really only a side interest and has assumed an importance quite out of proportion to the real significance of the *Diary*. That significance is this: that Parson Woodforde does for the country life of George III's reign—the life, that is to say, of the vast majority of our ancestors in that un-urban age—what Pepys does for London life in the reign of Charles II. In short, he illuminates the everyday detail of the time; he introduces us to a host of ordinary folk in all walks of life—except the aristocracy, though you will meet a number of bishops, a peer or two, a sprinkling of baronets, knights, and what not—you will meet, I say, all sorts and conditions of men, the kind of people who travelled by coach and on horseback down those delightful eighteenth-century turnpikes, who sat upon the magistrates' bench—when England really was ruled by Justices of the Peace, who ministered in elegiac churches, who ploughed the fields and harvested the hay smelling like a violet, who quarrelled and drank, who fell in love, who helped the poor with generous hand, who defended the country in dreaded times of French invasion, who went to Church once on a Sunday—if there was a service—and who, at last, were carried to their resting-places beneath the shadow and protection of the grey church towers in the lovely and immemorial villages of England.

Chapter Four

STILL GLIDES THE STREAM

A leading article in *The Times* of November 5th, 1932, opened with the words: "Next Thursday at the Green Man Hotel, in the Derbyshire town of Ashbourne, bids will be asked for one of the most beautiful strips of all England." The article ended with a strong plea that the National Trust should acquire Beresford Dale—"this place of smiling historic interest and supreme natural beauty." A week earlier, on October 28th, *The Times* photographer had surpassed himself by a view of Pike Pool crowned with autumnal trees, the river flowing on—just as old Walton described it—"through the most pleasant valleys and most fruitful meadows that this nation can justly boast of."

It is now twelve years since we visited Beresford Dale for the first time, in the summer of 1920, on pilgrimage to the ancestral shrine, and were made welcome by the phantoms:

> *Numerous as shadows haunting faerily*
> *The brain new stuffed with triumphs gay*
> *Of old romance.*

In particular my kinsman, Charles Cotton, seemed rather downcast that his poems had entered the world two years after his death in a form not at all pleasing to him, and suggested that a new edition might do more justice to his name. He appealed to his "Father" Walton, who very heartily agreed. With that I set to work, and with the help of the *London Mercury*, which published a long essay on Charles Cotton's poetry in November 1921, and of my friends Mr. Edmund Blunden and Mr. Richard Cobden-Sanderson the new edition was launched from Thavies Inn in May 1923.

Now, as this essay is one of ancestral gossip, and as I have a curiously strong feeling that dead men rise up ever, that time is all one, that past, present and future are intertwined by invisible filaments and that we are, at least a little, dream children, I will begin by telling the reader how Izaak Walton introduced me to his brother angler Parson Woodforde. From this visit to Beresford Dale, where Izaak Walton fished so often, I came away feeling on very intimate terms with the old man, who had been so good a friend to Charles Cotton. Two years later I was conversing with Parson Woodforde's great-great-great-nephew, Dr. R. E. H. Woodforde. The talk, Izaak Walton passing by at the moment, drifted to the author of the *Compleat Angler*. Whereupon my friend said that an ancestor of his, one the Reverend Doctor Samuel Woodforde, had known Walton at Winchester and written some dedicatory poems to him, that he had kept a diary, and that a great-grandson of Samuel's had also kept a diary which was of very great family interest to him, though he did not suppose it would interest the rest of the world, as being almost too domestic. I asked my friend to let me read this diary, and then and there he lent me the first of those neat little manuscript volumes which I read pretty steadily thereafter for seven years. The five printed volumes of *The Diary of a Country Parson: the Reverend James Woodforde, 1758–1802,* published by the Oxford University Press, are the result of that casual conversation, which in turn arose out of the visit to Beresford Dale in 1920.[1]

Moreover, Parson Woodforde himself introduced me to some of my mother's ancestors in Somerset, and to some lost cousins, and to a very large number of people in all parts of the world, practically from China to Peru. And now, late in 1932, the Dale has just emerged from a considerable ordeal. At the Green Man, Ashbourne, on November 10th, a syndicate of estate agents bid up to £15,250 for this radiant dominion of the Dove and were only overmastered by the bid of a local lover of the valley, Sir Ian Walker, who went £250 better. Failing the National Trust, and probably in any case in present circumstances, there could be no better owner. Sir Ian Walker writes to me to say that "from the public standpoint, the Dale will be preserved as in the past as a place of natural beauty for public enjoyment." And now, perhaps, the public will respond by *not* littering that loveliness with paper bags, or trespassing where they are not meant to go. The lower part

[1] It may be of interest to record that no less than three publishers rejected the first volume of the Woodforde *Diary* before the Oxford University Press accepted it. Presumably the other publishers rejected it because they thought it was too domestic to interest the general public. In point of fact it may, I think, be said that the publication of the Woodforde *Diary* has been largely responsible for creating a new interest in purely domestic records: certainly during the past ten or twelve years (the first volume of the Woodforde *Diary* appeared in 1924) the number of domestic journals and papers which have been printed is notable.

of the valley—Dove Dale proper—was at one time quite
disfigured by litter. Is that hideous menace weakening? We
will not wait for an answer at the moment, being in a
gossiping mood. And for those who visit the Dale now or
hereafter, or who like history in miniature, it may be of
use and of interest to string together a few scattered beads
which one may tell, if one pleases, in the chimney corner
in an idle hour.

Old Antiquary Erdeswicke is writing about his native
county of Staffordshire in the reign of our sovereign lady
Queen Elizabeth, and is describing the river Dove, his style
a little winding like the stream:

"Dove then takes its beginning at the Thrieshire Mear,
where the very spring stands, between Cheshire, Derbyshire, and Staffordshire, and so holds on its course through
a mountainous wild Country and hath neither Gentleman's
House nor good Town. For until it be past the Mountain
Country, the Bank is not of that estimation I have spoken
of, being very narrowly penn'd in with Mountains, so that
the name of that Bank for a good space is call'd Narrow
Dale. In the end whereof a Gentleman hath his Seat, the
place and the man having both the name of Beresford.
Edward Beresford hath now his Seat there; Edward was the
son of Sampson, the son of Robert, the son of John, the son
of John, which first John lived in Henry the 6th's time.

Dove being past Beresford leaveth Allstonfield, whereof
Beresford is a member, a mile westward."[1]

[1] Erdeswicke's *Survey of Staffordshire*, p. 172, edition of 1717. The
Survey was begun by Erdeswicke in 1594. He died in 1603. His home
was at Sandon.

138

The son of John, the son of John—Erdeswicke gets back
a hundred and fifty years to Henry VI's reign and then
gives it up. But he could have carried the story back to
Henry III's reign, and very explicitly to that of Edward I
and to the year 1275. The magnificent series of records
published by the William Salt Archæological Society,
entitled *Collections for a History of Staffordshire,* sweep away
the mists and mirages of time and show an English county
in all the detail of its many-coloured life through the
centuries, as far back, that is to say, as written records go.

In 1275, Edward I wished to know something about the
conditions of things in the Totmonslow Hundred of
Staffordshire. So he commanded that an Inquisition should
be held. Such things were accomplished in the immemorial
English way of a jury. The jurors who inquired included
Sir Philip de Draycote, Roger de Verney, Symon Bassett,
William Meverel in Ilam, Richard de Acovére (Oakover),
John de Beveresfort, and eight others. They report that
things are none too satisfactory. Three great lords—Henry
de Audley and Hugh le Despencer and Warine de Vernun
—have set up a gallows at Alstonfield: by what warrant
they—the jurors—know not. The Abbot of Deulacres and
the Lord of Altan are forcibly and unjustly taking passage
money from those who pass through their lands. The
Sheriff of the County takes money and conceals offences.
Henry, the Rector of the Church of Blore, took ten shillings
from William de Narrowdale. John Bareil had hidden
Robert Oviet for a mark, while William Rome had concealed his brother in his house at Alstonfield, though his

brother was an outlaw. The coroners are corrupt. These are some of the things which the jurors report.[1]

Thirty odd years pass by and the place named Beveresford,[2] in times beyond the reach of recorded history, has shortened itself for convenience sake, and assumes its present form. Soon the beavers will be altogether forgotten, and the owners of this dale of England will imagine that the place was connected somehow with bears: after all, wolves had given their name to the neighbouring Wolfscote. So a little later they choose a bear for their coat. Meanwhile an Inquisition in 1308 into the estate and heritage of one of the Audleys, who owned a third part of the Manor of Alstonfield, shows for what service or consideration Beresford Dale is held. The jurors say that there are various free tenants in Alstonfield and among them "Adam de Beresford, who holds the hamlet of Beresford for one quiver of arrows feathered, and two arrows bolted, price 8½d."[3] From the top of the precipice looking down on the Dove you can still hear the sharp hiss of arrows in the clean air, if you have ears to hear. These particular arrows, or money in lieu, were to be rendered annually to the chief lord upon the Feast of St. Michael the Archangel.

During the fourteenth century the men of the Dale serve in the Scottish and French wars as archers, stand surety for neighbours who are accused of violence, do a little

[1] *H.S.C.*, Vol. V (Old Series), Part I, pp. 117-21.
[2] It is named thus in a charter as old as 1228, witnessed by Hugo de Beveresford.—Ormerod's *Cheshire*, Vol. III, p. 495.
[3] *H.S.C.*, Vol. XI (New Series), pp. 256-7.

breaking into chases themselves, and defend their own lands from similar assaults. The country stretching between Alstonfield and Leek was forest, Malbanc Forest it was called; all around, indeed, were mountain and moor and forest. Between the valley of the Manifold and Beresford Dale a squirrel could leap from bough to bough.[1] The Beresfords held the office or offices—there seem to have been two—of foresters of the forest of Malbanc. As such they had rights of pasture therein for thirteen cows and a bull, thirteen mares and a horse, thirteen swine and a boar, besides various other useful privileges for domestic comfort in those stark times.

For the times were uncommonly stark and violent, and in the fifteenth century, and particularly during the reign of Henry VI, assaults and counter-assaults of many sorts and kinds were frequent. "The records of the period," as Mr. Trevelyan says in his *History of England*, "sometimes give a curious picture of a set of country gentlemen now enforcing the King's Peace and the Statutes of Labourers, now charged with robbery, piracy and murder, now sitting on the Bench, now sent to prison."[2] The general statement of the historian is amply confirmed by the particular records of Staffordshire, and as the vast panorama of history can only become really alive if one knows how a small part of the landscape actually looked, let us watch the sort

[1] *A History of the Manor of Beresford*, privately printed by the Rev. W. Beresford and S. B. Beresford, Part I, p. 10, and *passim*. I am deeply indebted to this scholarly work.

[2] G. M. Trevelyan's *History of England*, pp. 255-6.

141

of thing that was happening in or about the valley of the Dove.

Here is Squire Ralf Basset of Blore in the year 1450 presenting a most grievous petition—in vivid English too, not dog Latin—to be heard by the Justices *coram Rege*.

"Mekely besechith Rauf Basset Squier, that whereas John Cokayn of Assheburne in the Schire of Derby Squier, Thurstan Vernon late of Haddon in the same Schire Squier, William Cokayn of Assheburne of the same schire gentilman with other malicias persones" to the number of thirty with unknown numbers of other riotous persons "arraied with Jakkes, salettes, bowes, arrowes, swords, gleyves and boklers . . . come [came] the Thursday next before the fest of Alhalowene in the (28th) yere of the regne of oure soveraine lord the Kyng to the place of your seid besecher called Blore in the shire of Stafford to the entent to have murdered, slayn, maymed and beton youre seid besecher, his tenaunts and his servaunts, and for to brenne his howse . . . and had not John Curboun, Richard Bagot, and Henry Bradburne with others herying of this grete riot and route come thider to the entent for to se peas kept and for to entreate them to go thens they had brennyd the place of youre seid besecher," and though they went off that time, they turned up again the next night and on another day, so that your said beseecher dare "in no wyse be at home in his one house which shuld be his grete defence and tuicion." Please your wisdoms to consider of it, and let these riotous persons appear before the Justices of our Sovereign Lord "to answere to the seid orrible riottes, wronges, assaultes, trespasses and oppressions after the discretion of the said Justice."

Ralf Basset appeared in person, but the accused failed to appear, and though a jury subsequently assessed his damages at a considerable sum the court declined to give judgement then and postponed the case to the octaves of St. Hillary, and from thence to the morrow of St. John the Baptist, and from thence every term up to the end of the reign, Squire Basset presenting himself each time quite fruitlessly.[1]

The Bassets and Beresfords had intermarried towards the end of the fourteenth century, but, notwithstanding, quarrels broke out in the fifteenth. Ralf Bassett is again to the fore, and in the same year that he complained of the "orrible riottes" he sues "Sampson Meverelle, late of Throweley, Knight, and Isabella his wife, and John Beresford, of Beresford, gentilman, for breaking into his close at Blore, and carrying off 12 oxen and 12 cows, worth 20 marks, and for beating, wounding and ill treating his men servants, so that he lost their services for a length of time." The defendants failed to appear, and the Sheriff is ordered to produce them. So the record runs, but it appears that the case, in the week of Pentecost, had come before "Sampson Meverelle, Knight, Justice of the Peace"! And this same Sir Sampson three years earlier had been charged with attempting to ambush and to kill the Vicar of Ilam, on the Sunday, too, before the Feast of the Conversion of St. Paul. Some years later, in 1452, Sir Sampson Meverell and John Beresford (who had also been accused of harbouring three alleged murderers) are committed to the Marshalsea, appear

[1] *H.S.C.*, Vol. III (New Series), pp. 193–4.

in court, and then—triumphantly produce Letters Patent of the King, pardoning them![1]

The Dale could not support all its children indefinitely, and a younger brother of the John just named, called Thomas, after fighting in the French Wars, settled three miles over the border in Derbyshire. There he acquired lands at Newton Grange, Fenny Bentley and Mapleton, married an heiress out of Cheshire and had a family of sixteen sons and five daughters. From this enormous family, in due course, descended the branch which later rose to eminence in Ireland, and the more home-loving and less ambitious or less adventurous sons who clung on to the ancestral soil till the early nineteenth century, thereafter seeking such solace as they could find in the professions.

I have in my possession a deed in which the Abbot of the Monastery of St. Mary of Combremer (Combermere in Cheshire) in the year 1472 granted to Thomas[2] the use of "a certain grange of ours called Newton Grange in the County of Derby"; the rent to be paid twice yearly at the Feasts of St. Martin in the Winter, and the Nativity of St. John; on the death of any holder the best beast to be paid as first fruit; and if the monk or messenger appointed to receive the rent failed to receive it after forty days from any Feast, or if Thomas or his heirs "have not been of good behaviour towards us the aforesaid Abbot and Convent and our Successors," then the Abbot could resume the grange.

[1] *H.S.C.*, Vol. III (New Series), pp. 199–200 and 209–10.

[2] He was already at Newton as early as 1445. I have a deed of that date.

Thus Thomas and the Abbot covenanted together at "our Monastery of Combremer in our Chapter House, on the Eve of St. Andrew the Apostle in the twelfth year of the reign of King Edward IV, 1472."

A little later, in 1474,[1] Thomas died at a ripe old age and was buried in the church of Fenney Bentley, where some fifty or seventy years afterwards an alabaster monument of a very extraordinary kind was erected to his memory by his sons or grandsons. This altar tomb shows Thomas and his wife Agnes recumbent in their shrouds, the shrouds tied above the head and below the ankles. On the sides of the tomb are depicted the sixteen sons and five daughters, also in their shrouds. Bears rampant with armorial shield, and a cornice round the tomb adorned with drums and trumpets, breastplates and gauntlets, halberts and swords, afford some secular relief to this solemn memorial of the dead.

An epitaph, partly in English and partly in Latin, reminds the reader that he also is mortal:

"Here lyes the corps of Thomas Berisforde Esquire the Sonne of John Berisforde late Lorde of Berisforde in the Countie of Stafford Esquire and Agnes his wife the daughter and heire of Robert Hassall in the Countie of Chester Esquire who had issue XVI sonnes and five daughters. Thomas departed this life the XXth day of March in the yeare of our Lord God 1473 and Agnes departed this life the XVIth day of March in the yeare of

[1] Thomas died on March 20th, 1473, according to the old reckoning, which is 1474, according to ours. The old year ran from March 31st to March 31st.

our Lord God 1467. here also lyes the corps of Heughe
third Sonne of the sayd Thomas and Agnes

> As you now are soe once were wee
> And as wee are soe shall you bee."

Some rather remarkable Latin verses follow in praise of
Thomas; the second verse, after telling that he was a
generous, learned and loving man, cultivating the muses
and justice, records his military exploits, particularly at
Agincourt:

> *Militiae Excellens, strenuus dux, fortis, et audax,*
> *Francia testatur, curia testis Agen.*

But now silent, dissolved in dust he lies, for we are but
earth, a bubble, smoke, dust, a shadow; while we speak we
perish and suddenly vanish away, and so finally—

> *Si sapiens homo sis, disce memento mori.*[1]

It is probable that the Latin verses were originally composed by the learned and clerical brother among the sixteen
sons, James, who was Vicar of Chesterfield in 1484 and
subsequently also Vicar of Wirksworth and Canon Resi-
dentiary and Prebendary of Lichfield. He was one of the
principal among the early benefactors of St. John's College,
Cambridge, and I like to think that this grandson of the
wild and secluded Dale was one of the disciples and
patrons of the New Learning which was then dawning

[1] A full description of this tomb, which the pilgrim to Beresford Dale
should visit, in Fenny Bentley Church—the church is small and contains
many beautiful things—will be found in the Rev. J. C. Cox's *Notes on
the Churches of Derbyshire*, Vol. II, pp. 467–8.

upon the world. A copy of his foundation deed supplied
to me by the courtesy of the Master of St. John's College is
before me as I write, and brings one vividly back to Cambridge on February 12th, in the twelfth year of the reign of
King Henry VIII, 1520.

By this deed, James paid over to the Master and Fellows
and Scholars of St. John's the sum of £400 of "lawfull
money of England with the which said money the said
Maister felowes and scholars have purchased londes and
Tentes by the yerly value of twenty poundes to the use of
the said Maister Felowes and scholars and ther successoures
for evermore." This sum was to endow two fellowships and
two scholarships to be called "Beresford scolers." The two
Fellows and "disciples" to have "meate and drynk . . . and
also yerly ther chambers withyn the same college . . . and
Barbour and launder and to be discharged of cook and
butteler's wages and of all other annual charges of the said
college." The Fellows were to have five marks each a year
payable in sums of ten shillings at Easter, Midsummer,
Michaelmas and "at the ffest of Christmas," and over and
above these sums of ten shillings, a further thirteen
shillings and four pence at the "ffest of Mychalmas . . . for
ther subsidie and at the fest of Christmas . . . for their
gownes." All the privileges and powers of the other
Fellows were to be theirs equally. James and his nephew
Edward to nominate the two Fellows and scholars during
their life, and afterwards the Master and Fellows to nominate.
Primarily those to be nominated were to be of James's name
and kindred, secondly of the parishes of Chesterfield,

Wirksworth and Ashbourne in Derbyshire or Alstonfield in Staffordshire, and thirdly "to be naturally borne in the countie of Derby and Stafford, and for defaute of suche then the said Master felowes and scolars of the said college to chose the most able and apte of their discrecyon within the said Universitie of Cambridge." These "Beresford scolars to praye for James and Lawrence [James's brother] and other ther frendes." The deed is sealed with the seal of Lichfield Cathedral and with a bear rampant, being the seal of James Beresford. These fellowships and scholarships survived in the form designed by the founder until the middle of the last century, when a Universities' Royal Commission recommended that they should be thrown open to all candidates and be merged in the general endowments of the College.[1] But James Beresford's name is still remembered annually at the commemoration service of the Founders and Benefactors of St. John's: "Let us now praise famous men and our fathers that begat us."

Eight years before he founded the fellowships and scholarships at Cambridge, James had also founded a chantry in his native church of Fenny Bentley at the altar "of our blessed Lady the Virgin, St. Katheren and St. Anthony," a secular priest there to pray for the good and prosperous estate of the said King (Henry VIII) and his "most noble wife Katheren Quene of England," of James himself, of George, Earl of Shrewsbury, of the Reverend Father in God, Jeffry Blyth, Bishop of Lichfield and

[1] The last family holder was my great-uncle, the Rev. J. J. Beresford, Rector of Castor, father of Mr. J. D. Beresford, the novelist.

Coventry, "and all and singular the founder's brothers, sisters, cousins and friends whilst they lived and for their souls when they should be passed from this present life." He mentions all his numerous brothers and sisters by name, and his sisters' husbands and his brothers' wives.[1]

Having thus provided as well as he could for the intellectual welfare of the posterity of his brothers and sisters and neighbours for evermore on earth, and for as speedy a passage as might be for their souls and his own soul through Purgatory into Paradise, the Reverend James Beresford fell asleep on July 13th, 1520, and was buried in Lichfield Cathedral.[2]

Meanwhile the elder branch of the family, the owners of the Dale, prospered in a quiet way through the sixteenth century, acquiring more lands, acting as the King's Escheators for Staffordshire on occasion and still holding the ancestral forester-ships. The duty of the Escheator, be it said, was to administer the estates that escheated to the Crown, or those for which the Crown was responsible as guardian during a minority.[3] The wills in this century show how rapidly things are changing.[4] Thus John Beresford, dying in 1522, before any whisper of Reformation, is very solicitous

1 British Museum Add. MSS. 6671, ff. 110–11.

2 *The History and Antiquities of Lichfield*, by the Rev. Thos. Harwood, F.S.A., p. 241 (published 1806). See also Cox's *Churches of Derbyshire*, Vol. IV, p. 453 (footnote).

3 *H.S.C.*, Vol. XV (New Series), pp. 295–6, 300, and 302.

4 The wills in question, from which I quote, are printed in the Rev. W. Beresford's *History of the Manor of Beresford*, ch. viii.

for his soul, handing out money right and left, to St. Chad at Lichfield and St. Mary's Convent at Coventry; Sandon Church to have a vestment for the priest's singing of mass, Salt Church a cope, and Alstonfield Church ten shillings; the Abbot of Hilton, the Grey Friars of Stafford, and also the Austin Friars of the same, more money for Masses. A priest to be installed at Beresford for three years, his son Robert to find him his board and his executor his wage. "Also I will that VI pound of waxe be burnt about my sepulture." Much more pleasing is his solicitude for the poor, every woman and child to have "at my buriall a peny," and twenty "pour maides XX nobles to there mariage of the wch I have named VIII and the other XII by the discrecons of myn executors." Robert his heir to be well set up with oxen, cows, bull, horses, mares, wethers and ewes at Beresford Hall and to have eight "of the grete silver spoons with apostells and stuffe of householde" as inventoried. Sir John Aston, Knight, "mine especial good master," to be his general executor and to have a hundred shillings to buy him a horse. His servants James and Rob to have each a beast or two, the two maidens each a heifer, John Hole a beast, the miller also a beast (if he abide his year) and the nurse a heifer if she abide her year and every week four pence.

Seventy years later John Beresford's grandson, who enjoyed the odd Christian name of Sampson, dying in 1593, will simply bequeath his soul "to Almightie God my Maker and Redeemer," and his body to the earth "in such parte of Christian buriall as to my Executors shall seem expedient and meet." He has quietly accepted the Reformed Faith, and the wax torches will no longer light up the coffin, nor the priests and monks chant "Dirige" for the soul.[1] Wealth has come to him during the prosperous reign of Queen Elizabeth, and he thanks God for sending him in this world "goods, chattells, cattells and Household stuffe," plate and other things "farre above my deserts." Yet there is a link with earlier ages in the armour he bequeathes to his eldest son, Edward, "all my Armor to his owne use," a link which, though gradually becoming more and more tenuous, will last on for another hundred years before finally disappearing from military use and fashion.

With Edward Beresford, who dies in 1621, the elder line comes to an end in an heiress, Olive, who inherits the Dale and considerable estates in Derbyshire. For Edward married his cousin Dorothy of Fenny Bentley, also an heiress, though the male line of Thomas still continued to flourish sturdily at neighbouring Newton Grange and elsewhere. After all, with the sixteen sons of that veteran of Henry V and VI, much seed could be raised up in divers parts of the country, spreading over about this time also into Ireland.

Upon the Feast of St. Michael the Archangel, 1608, Olive Beresford, a girl not yet sixteen, was married to Sir John Stanhope of Elvaston in Fenny Bentley Church. Dr. Abbott, afterwards Bishop of Salisbury, preached the sermon from the text in the Book of Amos: "Can two walk together except

[1] "Dirige Domine Deus meus in conspectu tuo viam meam." (From the *Officium Defunctorum*, Roman Breviary.)

they be agreed?" Six years later Olive died in giving birth to another Olive.[1]

Michael Drayton commemorated her in an elegy—"Upon the Death of the Lady Olive Stanhope." The poet must have been invited either by Sir John or her father to compose the elegy, for he says he had never seen her, though she evidently admired his poetry:

> *Me thou didst love unseene, so did I thee,*
> *It was our spirits that loved then, and not wee;*
> *Therefore without profaneness I may call*
> *The love betwixt us, love spirituall.*
>
> . . . . . .
>
> *Thy shape and beauty often have to me*
> *Bin highly praysed, which I thought might be,*
> *Truely reported, for a spirit so brave,*
> *Which heaven to thee so bountifully gave.*
>
> . . . . . .
>
> *Let not the world report then, that the Peake,*
> *Is but a rude place only vast and bleake.*

He ends with some pleasant rhetoric about the wonders of the Peak and how Olive excels them all:

> *Let her account thee greatest, and still to time*
> *Of all the rest, accord thee for the prime.*[2]

[1] The first Olive was baptised on December 29th, 1592, and died January 29th, 1613–14. Charles Cotton the elder, who eloped with the second Olive, said she was then under sixteen, and as their son was born in 1630, I deduce that Olive, Lady Stanhope, died in childbirth. *A History of the Manor of Beresford*, p. 79, and Glover's *Derbyshire*, Vol. II, pp. 48–9.

[2] From Drayton's *Elegies upon Sundry Occasions* included in the 1627 edition of his works and reprinted in *Minor Poems of Michael Drayton*, edited by Cyril Brett (Clarendon Press, 1907, pp. 116–18).

The second Olive now became heiress of the Dale and of Fenny Bentley and the other acres, and, until her grandfather Edward died in 1621, she seems to have lived with him. In his will he bequeathes £20 to Olive's nurse Ann Lant, "for her paines taken with my grandchild, trusting shee will be as carefull of her bringing upp during her service as formerly shee hath." Whether Ann Lant interpreted her trust in the liberal spirit of Juliet's nurse we do not know, but certain it is that before Olive had attained the age of sixteen she had managed to elope with the Romeo of her time. It suffices to say that while she was staying in London at her father's— Sir John Stanhope's—house in Salisbury Court, she was sought out by Charles Cotton—"a gentleman . . . so qualified in his person and education, that for many years he continued the greatest ornament of the town, in the esteem of those who had been best bred." So Lord Clarendon thought, and there can be no better judge.

Charles Cotton, who was then about twenty-five,[1] was told of Olive's attractions, and, having satisfied himself, he says, by "the sight of her person," he arranged to meet her at the house of one of her aunts. Very rapidly he disclosed his feelings for her, which she returned with equal ardour. So he moved her in the way of marriage. But she said, through messages passed between them, that the only way to manage the affair would be "by carrying of her away, and did herself appoint to come to this Defendant if he could come for her." All this Romeo explains very exactly in a legal document which he later drew up, when Sir John

[1] He went up to Cambridge in 1618, probably aged about fourteen.

Stanhope haled him before the Court of Star Chamber. So he prepared a coach, came near to Salisbury Court, and Olive of her own accord stepped into the coach and "went away with this Defendant and the same night this Defendant confesseth that they were married together and ever since cohabited together as Husband and Wife."

Passion and fervency of affection transported him, Charles Cotton afterwards told Sir John Stanhope, who had roundly accused him of conspiracy and riot and perjury and unlawful practices. The truth seems to have been that Sir John had made all arrangements to marry Olive to someone else, and that Olive and Charles very rightly determined otherwise. And though, in after years, they drifted apart, all the brave morning of their love was triumphantly vindicated by the birth of the poet, Charles Cotton the younger. As he was born in April 1630, his mother was barely sixteen, for Charles the elder protests that at the time of the elopement he did not know that "the said Olive was under the age of sixteen years, but was credibly informed she was of the age of above sixteen years."[1] It is clear that the elopement took place in 1629, because, years afterwards, when unhappiness had come, Olive, in an appeal to the House of Lords, dated 1647, herself says that "about eighteen years since she did in her extream affection marry her now husband," to whom she had brought great possessions, though now he neglected her.

[1] The legal document from which I have quoted so freely will be found in the Introduction to my edition of Charles Cotton's poems, published by R. Cobden-Sanderson in 1923. Since then the document, with other family papers, has passed into my possession, and I have here corrected one or two verbal errors by reference to the original MS.

154

Olive died in her thirty-eighth year, in 1651, and was buried in Fenny Bentley Church. Her cousin, the poet, Sir Aston Cockayne, lamented her in an epitaph:

> *One only son she left, whom we presage*
> *A grace t'his family, and to our age.*
> *She was too good to live, and young to die,*
> *Yet stay'd not to dispute with destiny. . . .*[1]

Her husband, who died in 1658, managed to dissipate a considerable part of his wife's wealth, but the poet, his son, still inherited a fair estate. And the elder Cotton, who had known all the wits and poets of his time, including Dr. Donne and Herrick and Lovelace and Wotton, when he looked back on his and Olive's romance perhaps murmured with his dying breath the magic words which Browning caught three centuries later:

> *And stood by the rose-wreathed gate. Alas,*
> *We loved, sir—used to meet:*
> *How sad and mad and bad it was—*
> *But then, how it was sweet!*

With the birth of Charles Cotton, the poet, we come to the time when Beresford Dale was to be made famous. And as the story of Charles Cotton's life and works and his friendship with Izaak Walton have long since become part of literary history we will not repeat it. Suffice it to say that, for him, the Dale was an earthly paradise, and the silver Dove a celestial stream winding in and out of his poetry and prose almost till the day of his early death in 1687.

[1] Sir Aston Cockayne's *Poems*, 1658.

Almost, but in the last years of his life he was compelled to sell Beresford Hall—in 1681. It was bought by John Beresford,[1] his neighbour and cousin, and Cotton seems still to have lived on there till within a year or two of his death. His celebrated translation of Montaigne's *Essays* was evidently completed there, for the great Lord Halifax, to whom it was dedicated in 1685, writes a charming letter of gratitude addressed "This for Charles Cotton, Esq., at his house at Beresford, to be left at Ashbourne, in Derbyshire." The gratitude of the noble Marquis, than whom there was hardly a better judge living of what was excellent in literature, must have warmed the cockles of the translator's heart:

"You have the original strength of his [Montaigne's] thought, that it almost tempts a man to believe the transmigration of souls, and that his being used to hills, is come into the Moorlands, to reward us here in England, for doing him more right than his country will afford him. He hath by your means mended his first edition. . . . You see, sir, I have kindness enough for Monsieur de Montaigne to be your rival; but nobody can now pretend to be in equal competition with you . . . pray believe, that he who can translate such an author without doing him wrong, must not only make me glad, but proud of being his very humble servant, HALIFAX."[2]

[1] John Beresford (1654–1724) of Ashbourne and Newton Grange, my grandfather to the fourth great, one of the Deputy Lieutenants for Derbyshire in the reign of Queen Anne. A good many letters from him have been published in the *Melbourne Manuscripts* by the Historical Manuscripts Commission.

[2] See the "Life of Charles Cotton" in Sir Harris Nicholas's exhaustive 1836 edition of *The Compleat Angler,* Vol. I, pp. cxciv–v.

We will end this essay with some letters, or parts of letters, hitherto unpublished, which will illustrate as only letters can, how deeply Beresford Dale and the Dove have twined themselves round the memories of men here and beyond the ocean.

In 1815, a very pleasant publisher, Mr. Samuel Bagster, and Mr. (afterwards Sir) Henry Ellis, of the British Museum, collaborated in producing an edition of *The Compleat Angler*. In the preceding year they both visited Beresford Dale, and the first letter is one from Mr. Bagster to Mr. Ellis, recounting how he (Mr. Bagster) had improved on his colleague's route to the spot, for they had gone there separately.

Mr. S. Bagster to Mr. Henry Ellis, letter dated from Buxton, September 21, 1814.

DEAR SIR,

I am now on my way from Berisford Hall to Chesterfield and Alfreton and propose to visit Ashbourne and to meet Mr. Linnell [Mr. John Linnell, R.A., the distinguished artist and patron of William Blake, who was commissioned to make a drawing of the Hall for the 1815 edition of *The Compleat Angler*] there on my way to London via Oxford.

My gratification has been very great; I expected much and it has in no degree disappointed me. I have trodden the whole way that Cotton pourtrays and such was his accuracy of delineation [in Part II of *The Compleat Angler*] that I have been confident of the *very spot* he is describing and can almost take on me to say that it is not five yards to the right or left that I fixed on——

The way that you directed by turning off at the 5m stone

157

is full 2 miles about, neither is it the road that Cotton went. I shall be happy to explain the reasons that induce me to entertain this opinion when I have the pleasure of seeing you—I turned off at 1 mile [from Ashbourne] which led me by Bentley Brook over the *old* Turnpike Road to Hanson Grange and Hanson Toot. Hanson Grange is a Farm the property of Mr. Wm. Gold on whom I called and with whom I spent a most agreable hour and who did very politely after tea accompany me on the way to point out the proper bridle road towards the hill leading to the *little* Bridge; from him I learn that the two fields between his house and the hill are called "the Toots" and therefore the name "Hanson Toots"—— It is worthy of remark that Cotton names particularly this spot, no doubt because of its peculiar fertility, for they are the two finest fields for miles; so does he, whenever he calls the attention of his friend, choose a place that has durable attractions, for those he has named present *at this time* more to admire than the surrounding scenes—— Although I have taken the liberty to suppose my way to Berisford Hall was Cotton's road you may be assured it was after I had pursued your directions with close attention. I first walked your road, I returned a different way and on my next jaunt to the Hall *my* way I found every place *exactly* coincide with his descriptions—— One thing I feelingly lament that the owner of the Hall should have cut down above 200 fulgrown Sycamore, Lime and Elm Trees, they constituted the riches of the Estate, the beauty of the scenery and the protection of the House: at present the young trees disfigure the scene, they neither shelter nor ornament and cause an observer more to feel the loss of the majestic trees that have been felled; two or three are left, to display the want of taste or want of money of the person who issued the destructive order——

On my way yesterday to the seat of the Cottons I was overtaken in Narrowdale Hill with a most severe storm and having spent too much time at good farmer Gold's it had brought on night. We determined therefore to walk back to Horsfield and there found comfortable quarters "in Lavender Sheets," though with very plain fare—— What can you let us have for supper? "We *kip* nothing but Bacon, sir, but we will give you Pikelets in the morning." This honest man's father valued the goods at the Hall in Mrs Osborne's time, who possessed the remains of Mr. Cotton's goods: take a specimen:

> Blue Chamber—6 armed chairs 6/-, 3 other chairs 3/6.
> 4 Pictures 4d.
> Little Parlour—2 Pictures no value—Pr. of Bellows 8d.
> Study—Writing Desk 1/6.

I have been aided in my endeavour to trace the footsteps of Cotton by the information and company of Mr. Jebb, the brother of the owner of the Hall[1] who has politely offered to accomodate Mr. Linnell with a bed etc as long as he may feel it desirable to remain in the neighbourhood and I am to meet that Gent^n. tomorrow in Chesterfield and I hope to obtain something that shall forward the object for which I am on this spot—— It will give me pleasure

[1] John Beresford and his son (also John) sold Beresford Hall in 1722, I suppose, because it was rather out of the way to live in. It was in various hands between then and 1825, when it was bought by Viscount Beresford (Wellington's Peninsular General). From him it passed to his stepson Beresford-Hope, whose son sold the property early in the present century. The Hall was pulled down in 1856: it was then in a hopeless state of disrepair.

to find that the effect of your recent close attention has been removed by the society of Tunbridge Wells; that seems a spot that must make everyone affable, the portraits of Pope and Richardson give this idea to me. Respectful remembrance to Mrs. Ellis. I am Sir

Your obed. and sin. svt.

S. BAGSTER.

In the autumn of 1848, Mr. Samuel Bagster was turning over some old papers. He was getting on in years, but the memory of the expedition of 1814, and its associations, came flooding back upon him and he felt impelled to write to his old companion, who was now Sir Henry Ellis, since 1827 Principal Librarian of the British Museum.

Mr. S. Bagster to Sir Henry Ellis, letter dated from The Cottage, Old Windsor: October 25th, 1848.

MY DEAR SIR,

The travelling instructions you obligingly gave me in 1814 when about to visit Berisford Hall are now before me and it is a real pleasure, after the stream of time has run 24 [he means 34] yrs to know that you continue actively fulfilling the intellectual duties of your important station.

At present, finding leisure to review the hints and materials I collected on that visit and subsequently, I feel inclined to narrate events in the order in which they occurred, but whether for the amusement of my children in MS or to be printed will be controlled by others better qualified to judge than myself——

In looking over these materials pleased am I to hope they are well adapted to form an interesting volume when joined with a new edition of the Complete Angler——

Still glides the Stream

Amongst other matters of less value I possess a full letter from C. Cotton to good Isaac in perfect preservation—clear and free from defect. This relic I much value and additional[ly] value by the channel through which it came to my hands—— On the back of this letter is a page of a sermon in the hand-writing of Mr. Walton Junr. Enclosed is a copy of Mr. Cotton's letter written in a rough manner but if your Walton Collectanea induce you to prefer a copy to be written more fair and on paper of any other size my pen is your willing instrument. . . . [Unfortunately the copy was not attached, and I have not been able to trace this letter of Cotton's.]

With the solemn remembrance that the several gentlemen who on my visit shewed me every possible courtesy are deceased (except one Joseph Jebb Esq.) I diffidently venture to express the hope that I shall have the pleasure to hear that your Lady as well as yourself are in the enjoyment of a happy measure of good health——

Since my visit I have to lament the removal of Philip Gell Esq., the Rev. Bache Thornhill, Mr. Gould, Mr. Langford, the Rev. H. C. Morewood and John Beresford Esqre.

I have the pleasure and honour to subscribe myself

Your faithful and obed. Sevt.

SAMUEL BAGSTER.[1]

Reader, I will end this mild gossip with a letter from Ohio which I received in 1925, from an unknown but very

[1] These letters were very kindly sent to me by Mr. H. J. Ellis, grandson of Sir Henry Ellis, together with the latter's MS. diary, part of which was published in an appendix to my edition of Charles Cotton's poems in 1923.

charming correspondent who had acquired *The Poems of Charles Cotton*. In the course of his letter he says:

"My first interest in Charles Cotton sprang from the fact that I have a rather worn and battered copy of the *Compleat Angler*, 1676 edition, inherited through many generations in my grandmother's family since some of them lived in the vicinity. I well remember when I found the old volume, a rummaging small boy living on the shores of Otsego Lake in New York state, and bore the treasure to show to this grandmother. She was very old—approaching 90—but as I turned the leaves and read the description of Pike Pool in Beresford Dale—' 'Tis a rock' etc, her old eyes glowed, and she told me of seeing the very place when a child in England over 70 years before. And when in 1922, just a century after her coming to America, my sister and I visited England for the first time, we went at once to Ashbourne, and our first English day was spent in walking from Hartington through the Dales to Thorpe."

.   .   .   .

Still glides the stream, and shall for ever glide.

So Wordsworth wrote of the river Duddon. But that immortal line applies to the Dove equally well, and indeed to all rivers, including the river of life.

Chapter Five

POETRY AND AGE

When Mr. Housman's book, *Last Poems*, was published in 1922 the critics naturally received it with the welcome which was its due. Mr. Housman was then past sixty years of age, and one of the reviewers—if my memory serves me right, and as I made a note at the time it is hardly likely to have served me wrong—observed that the author was "a young man" when he published his first and famous book *The Shropshire Lad*. This observation drew a comment from someone who had read the review in question, to the effect that it was hardly correct to describe Mr. Housman as a young man—"as youth is usually reckoned in poets." The commentator was right in part of his comment, for *The Shropshire Lad* was written for the most part—so the author himself tells us—in the early months of 1895, when he was thirty-six years of age. But in correcting a minor error the commentator fell into a major one, for he seems to imply that youth and poetry are peculiarly linked—"as youth is usually reckoned in poets," he says.

Well! How is youth reckoned in poets? My impression is that it is frequently reckoned wrong. There is a pretty widespread notion that poetry is predominantly associated with youth, is almost the private property of youth, that the great poets, in short, produced their best work in that golden time. It is a mistake. The best poetry has been, in fact, for the most part the product of prosaic middle age· and beyond.

Though this assertion will be found to be generally justified, we must begin our attack by a surrender of some very rich ground. Keats died when he was twenty-four, Shelley on the threshold of thirty, Byron when he was thirty-six. Coleridge wrote his best poetry before he was thirty. Burns came out with his Kilmarnock edition of poems when he was twenty-seven. So there is some substance for the heresy about youth. Nevertheless, it is, in the main, a heresy. And even in the case of the poets just named—with the exception of Coleridge, whose inspiration simply languished—it is impossible to say whether loftier flights would not have followed. Their careers illustrate the truth, which no one would question, that great poetry can be written in youth, not that youth is the mainspring of the greatest poetry.

And now let the tide of time flow back with us. We must keep to our own country, for space is brief and the theme widespread. Nevertheless, by way of European challenge, let us observe that *The Divine Comedy* was conceived when Dante describes himself as "in the midway of this our mortal life," and that *Faust* spans almost all Goethe's fourscore years—youth, middle, and old age.

Chaucer's greatest work, *The Canterbury Tales*, was the work of his later years. Definite dates are lacking, but Professor Skeat suggests that the work was begun when

Chaucer was forty, and it was not apparently completed when the poet died at the age of sixty or over.

Spenser's *Faerie Queene* begins to make its appearance when Spenser was thirty-seven, and is not completed till he was forty-four. Moreover, the four supreme hymns, the *Amoretti* sonnets, and the *Epithalamium* are all the work of a middle-aged man.

We come to the world figure of poetry. All Shakespeare's greatest work was done after he was thirty, including the Sonnets. From that time on the Plays are in a *crescendo* of magnificence. Shakespeare died when he was fifty-two, and into the seventeen years between 1595 and 1612 are crowded the great majority of the Plays. *Hamlet* is the work of a man—or an angel—on the borders of forty; *Othello*, *Macbeth*, *King Lear*, *Antony and Cleopatra* follow; *Cymbeline*, *The Tempest*, and the *Winter's Tale* come with their crown of tranquillity.

By common consent the next figure to Shakespeare is Milton. The greatest epics in the English language were the work of a man on the threshold of old age. Milton was born in 1608. *Paradise Lost* was published in 1667. It was begun some years before, and the date of the beginning is placed in the year 1658. Seven years later it was ready for the press, but the Plague and the Fire delayed publication for another two years. *Paradise Regained* was published in 1671. Milton's latest editor, Mr. E. H. Blakeney, suggests with good reason that Milton dictated *Paradise Regained* between 1665 and 1667 and then revised it. *Samson Agonistes* is assigned to the immediately following years. It is true that most of the shorter poems, including *L'Allegro* and *Il Penseroso*, *Comus* and *Lycidas* were written before he was thirty. But relatively to the Epics these—to adapt a famous metaphor which Wordsworth used of his own poetry—are but the porches to a vast cathedral, of which *Samson Agonistes* is the high altar.

> *Thy soul was like a star, and dwelt apart;*
> *Thou hadst a voice whose sound was like the sea,*
> *Pure as the naked heavens, majestic, free.*

So Wordsworth saluted Milton, and has himself been placed by Matthew Arnold next to Milton in the poetic firmament. Arnold's order is Shakespeare, Milton, Wordsworth. Not many students of poetry would dispute this order, and, as the years go by, the star of Wordsworth shines with an increasing lustre.

And again it is true of Wordsworth, as of the others, that his best work is not the work of his youth. Wordsworth was born in 1770, and his main poems of genius—with the great exception of *Tintern Abbey*—were produced between 1800 and 1820. Within this period of his life, between thirty and fifty, come all the finest separate sonnets, the famous *Ode on Intimations of Immortality*, by far the greater part of *The Prelude* and *The Excursion*, and the prolonged series of sonnets. To the disciple of Wordsworth *The Prelude* and *The Excursion*, almost epical in length, are what he himself regarded them, his main work: they contain his life, his philosophy and great stretches of supreme poetry. He was fifty when he wrote the final sonnet of the Duddon series, one of the most splendid in the English language:

166

> *I thought of Thee, my partner and my guide,*
> *As being past away.—Vain sympathies !*
> *For, backward, Duddon! as I cast my eyes,*
> *I see what was, and is, and will abide.*

Of the successors of Wordsworth, the great Victorians, the case equally holds, that the main part of their best work was accomplished after they attained the age of thirty and within the period of the middle years, and later still. This is true of Browning and Tennyson, the two chief figures.

Within our own time and memory there come *The Dynasts* begun by Thomas Hardy in 1897, when he was fifty-seven, and completed ten years later. And hot-foot within the last few years—in 1929—there is *The Testament of Beauty* to bear witness how fourscore years may mount up with wings as eagles, can run and not be weary, walk and not faint.

And now, Reader, I will end by asking you whether the lines that follow were written in youth or middle age, and if you answer rightly you will agree with me that youth is certainly very well, but that age or middle age have even more to be said for them than it has been possible to say in so brief a space.

> *Love, lift me up upon thy golden wings,*
> *From this base world unto thy heaven's Hight,*
> *Where I may see those admirable things,*
> *Which there thou workest by thy soveraine might,*
> *Farre above feeble reach of earthly sight,*
> *That I thereof an heavenly Hymne may sing*
> *Unto the god of Love, high heaven's King.*

Chapter Six

SUMMER: 1782

No doubt it was very like other Summers—that is to say like other Summers which deserve that lovely name, having disentangled themselves altogether from the cold clutches of Winter. But to one person at least it was supremely memorable: to him the English meadows in June, the rounded hills, the clear streams, appeared with the radiance and the peace of Paradise. "In the vale below, flocks were feeding; and from the hills, I heard the sweet chimes of distant bells."

It is eight years since I last read that tranquil sentence, and picking up the book again it still has all the freshness of the first reading, which means that he who wrote it wrote with sincerity and truth. It is Pastor Carl Moritz who is writing, in high June of 1782, and those who have not yet read his *Travels through Several Parts of England* in that year, have some hours of unclouded joy before them.[1] Strange he must have looked, plodding along the road between Richmond and Oxford, for he had chosen to walk in order to see England better—the country he had always so longed to visit, the land which had produced not only Shakespeare

1 Published by the Oxford University Press in the Miscellany Series, with an Introduction by P. E. Matheson, price 3s. 6d.

but his beloved Milton. Every now and again he would pause, seek out a shady part of the hedge, take from the voluminous pocket of his skirted coat a well-used copy of *Paradise Lost* and bury himself in the original Garden of Eden. Then he would look up and gaze at the enchanting landscape: if such scenes as lay stretched before him existed anywhere in Germany they would be deemed a Paradise, he thought. Nor was it merely the landscape which delighted Pastor Moritz. Though not himself a Prussian, he had spent a good many years in Berlin as a teacher, and the absolutely un-militaristic aspect of England gave him unfeigned pleasure. "No walls, no gates, no sentries, nor garrisons," he murmurs. "No stern examiner comes here to search and inspect us, or our baggage; no imperious guard here demands a sight of our passports: perfectly free and unmolested, we here walk through villages and towns, as unconcerned, as we should through an house of our own." Only, as he passed through rural Kensington *en route* for Richmond—from which he began his walk—he noticed that the travellers on the coach had been disagreeable and haughty to a Jew, and observes that the antipathy to Jews was more marked in England than in Germany. But this was in 1782.

As he walked along from Richmond to Oxford his main difficulty was the inns, obtaining a night's rest therein. It appears that our insular ancestors found it hard to understand why anyone should walk who could afford to ride. The peaceful and respectable pastor trudging along in the burning sun, his dark coat freely besprinkled with dust from the coaches and post-chaises which rattled past, and his face streaming with sweat, was no welcome guest at the grander inns, and even the simple wayside ones hesitated to take in so eccentric a traveller. Sometimes he was compelled to move on, dead-beat, though in the end he always succeeded in finding a night's lodging. One must have had a heart of stone to turn from the door that weary figure, the honest and innocent eyes gazing at one so pleasantly and so beseechingly! At any rate the host of the inn at Nettlebed, some miles beyond Henley—Henley was too fine a place for him to stop at—could not turn the good pastor away. We are still grateful to that host, and trust that his spirit even now walks the earth and comforts, unseen, poor travellers on the way.

For it was in Nettlebed village that Pastor Moritz passed one of the happiest days of his life: so happy, indeed, that we ourselves are made at once to share his vivid joy, expressed with the true simplicity of genius. It was late on Saturday night, June 22nd, 1782, that he reached the inn at Nettlebed and entered the hospitable kitchen with its array of pewter, the joints roasting before the fire, and the great flitches of bacon, the sugar-loaves and the hams suspended from the ceiling. And so, after a good meal, to bed in a comfortable, carpeted room. He made himself so smart with a change of clean linen in the morning that the inn people showed him into the parlour instead of the kitchen, and called him by the more respectful "Sir," instead of the mere "Master" reserved for simpler folk.

It was Sunday, and Pastor Moritz saw the village boys drawn up to wait for the parson—their hair combed on the

171

forehead, "their bosoms open, and the frills of their shirts turned back on each side": presently the parson arrived on horseback, and everyone bowed very low and went into the church. And there Pastor Moritz was infinitely edified by the congregation and the choir, with musical instruments, striking up the 47th Psalm:

> *O clap your hands together, all ye people:*
> *O sing unto God with the voice of melody.*
>
> *For the Lord is high, and to be feared:*
> *He is the great King upon all the earth.*

The pastor was much affected by the liturgy of the Church of England, by the congregation joining in prayer and by the music so "calculated to raise the heart to devotion." All that Sunday he remained at Nettlebed. "I seemed indeed to be enchanted, as if I could not leave this village. Three times did I get off, in order to go on farther, and as often returned. . . ."

Away down in Somerset in this pleasant month of June 1782, Parson Woodforde was staying with Sister Pounsett at Cole. He and Nancy had set out from Norwich on May 29th, and leaving Mr. Du Quesne, who had come with them as far as London to stay with the Archbishop of Canterbury at Lambeth, had journeyed on into the west by the Salisbury coach. On the same Sunday that Pastor Moritz visited Nettlebed Church, Parson Woodforde attended service in Pitcomb Church, and "as we came back from the Church we stopped by a very fine Spring in Pitcomb Street in which I threw a Shilling for the Boys there to scramble for.

We also called in at Taylor Wilmot's and drank some of his Ale—I gave his comical Maid Nan o.1.o."

.   .   .   .

On this June day, Whit Sunday of 1933, as I sit writing by the open door, looking out at the garden and beyond the garden to a field filled with buttercups—the cows dozing in the hot sun—I wonder whether things have changed very much in the last one hundred and fifty years, or whether fundamentally they are very much the same. There are still immemorial villages and clean springs for boys to scramble for shillings in; still chime the bells, and the calm liturgy of the Church of England maintains its ancient beauty; the chaffinches and the yellow-hammers sing for ever their monotonous and lovely song from the hedgerows sprayed with wild roses; the meadows by the stream and the patterned fields on the hillside glow beneath the radiant sun of June, and all the air is musical with the drowsy hum of bees.

I see the shadowy figure of Pastor Moritz leaning over the gate which leads into the buttercup field of beaten gold; still he lingers there, entranced by the tranquillity of the scene before him; his lips move, and the serene words which he is whispering over to himself weave themselves into the breeze:

"But thy eternal summer shall not fade."

Chapter Seven

ON BEING CONTENT

He could not quite remember how old he was, my neighbour of the long white beard, who inhabited one of the pleasant houses looking out on the long village street. He thought he was seventy-eight, but his cheerful daughter corrected him: "No, Father," she said, "you are eighty-six, and shortly going to be eighty-seven!" "Ay! Ay!" he said, "it is so." We relapsed into silence for a moment, and the daughter, who was cooking some eminently delicious scones on a girdle, offered to go. But I would by no means consent. It is not every day that one can sit in a small cosy kitchen, and watch a spectacle so pleasing—the rounded flour cake becoming, by degrees almost imperceptible, tinged with a faint brown, when it was taken off quietly and another put in its place.

The old man said he had little to complain of: he could still read, though his eyes sometimes gave trouble. Still they were, perhaps, better than in his youthful days, when he had been decidedly short-sighted.

In his youthful days, where had he lived? In Scotland, in one of the Highland counties. On Sunday one went to church at about 11.15 in the morning, and came out again at about 4.15 p.m.: a half-hour interval in between, when, if you were discreet, you munched bread and cheese. Were they exhausted by such inordinate length of sermon and service—at least an hour for the sermon? He thought not, remembering how his father leaned forward with ear cocked towards the preacher, wishing to miss nothing of the discourse. The children, moreover, on Sunday were expected to learn several verses of the metrical psalms and had to repeat them to their father.

"What happened," said I, "if you failed to learn your verses?" "We never did," replied the old man instantly, at which we both broke into prolonged laughter, as the way in which he said it called into the room the image of that solemn, kindly father, stern withal, whom to offend in such a way was simply unthinkable. This father walked to his work four or five miles over a pathless moor every morning, and was clearly not a man to be trifled with, and *his* father before him had had various experiences with excise men in the days when one distilled whisky on the quiet, and resented official interference.

"What was the house like," I asked, "in which you were brought up?" "A two-roomed farmhouse," he replied, "and the beds were box-beds, entirely closed in the day, entered by a door at night, through which the air came. The mattresses were filled with chaff." But the conditions of the eighteen-fifties were so entirely different to those of to-day that the old man was simply incapable of describing them. "And yet," he said, "no one thought of them as hardships."

We talked about Walter Scott, whose poetry he liked, but

176

he was quick to add that Burns was the real idol of the peasantry of Scotland, and that Scott had never taken with them as Burns had. It was now time for me to leave my venerable friend, and as I walked home I pondered over those words: "And yet no one thought of them [those austere conditions of the old man's youth] as hardships."

To some extent, of course, we none of us think of the old-fashioned days of our youth as times of hardship: we like to try and delude our children into thinking how heroic we were: ice-cold hip-baths and what not. But, in fact, they were not hardships, for we knew of nothing better, and it is in the mind that we are thus and thus. Still, two rooms, and box-beds, and pathless moors, particularly if deep in snow and swept with wintry blasts—these things can only be enjoyed by the strong in body and the contented in spirit. Moreover, things can be endured in the country which are unendurable in the town.

But the real truth, no doubt, is the very trite one that we may be content with very little, and that too much simply distracts. I turn up my *Compleat Angler* and hear peaceful Piscator discoursing to the Scholar, as they walk through the meadows:

"Let me tell you, Scholar, that Diogenes walked on a day with his friend, to see a country fair; where he saw ribbons, and looking-glasses, and nut-crackers, and fiddles, and hobby horses, and many other gimcracks; and having observed them and all the other finnimbrans that make a complete country fair, he said to his friend, 'Lord, how many things are there in this world of which Diogenes hath no need?' And truly," adds Piscator, "it is so, or might be so, with very many who vex and toil themselves to get what they have no need of."

But there is one very important, though it may not be essential, element in being content which even Diogenes certainly found necessary: I mean books, or their equivalent. And that reminds me that my old friend with the white beard had mentioned Scott and Burns in his talk, and I do not doubt that his faculty of reading by the fireside, now that he can no longer stride forth into the fields, helps to maintain tranquillity of mind. So, at least, would have agreed Izaak Walton's cheerful friend and brother angler, Charles Cotton, who, celebrating "contentation" in one of his poems and describing the happy man, sings with his clear voice:

> *"That man is happy in his share,*
> *Who is warm clad, and cleanly fed,*
> *Whose necessaries bound his care,*
> *And honest labour makes his bed.*
>
> .   .   .   .   .
>
> *Who with his angle, and his books,*
> *Can think the longest day well spent,*
> *And praises God when back he looks,*
> *And finds that all was innocent."*

Chapter Eight

TAKING THE ROAD

Let us take the Road!
Hark! I hear the sound of Coaches!

Gay's famous song in the *Beggar's Opera*, though two centuries have gone by, loses none of its freshness to-day when the whole world takes the road. On bicycles and in 'buses, in coaches, charabancs, and motor-cars of every sort and size the citizens of 1930 stream along the highways and the byways of their England.

Of all the changes which have taken place in the last one hundred and fifty years none is more startling than the revolution in the means and method of travel. And yet, if you think of the 1780's as the birthday of your great-grandfather, it does not seem so far off. After all, he only died some seventy years ago, and your father could remember him well enough!

Look back, for a moment, into this England of the late eighteenth century. On May 16th, 1778,

"about seven o'clock this evening who should arrive at my house in a Post-Chaise and Pair, but Mr Pounsett and Sister Pounsett. . . ."

It is Parson Woodforde of Weston, Norfolk, who is chatting in his *Diary*: he goes on:

"They had come that day 100 miles. They set out from Ansford (Somerset) on Wednesday morn' last, and they came by way of London and in a Post Chaise all the way from London. They were much tired. . . ."

As seven miles an hour—allowing for changing horses, turnpikes, and halts—represented "good going" in those days, it is safe to assume that Parson Woodforde's guests had been up between four and five in the morning, if not earlier. No wonder they were tired! Not that this feat of endurance was by any means unique. When Wesley was an old man of eighty-six he travelled eighty miles and preached at the end of the journey: this is how he describes it in his *Journal* for August 6th, 1789:

"We set out early, and between four and five reached Hinxworth (Hertfordshire). I was now pretty well inclined to rest; but a congregation soon getting together, I would not disappoint them, but preached on 'We love him because he first loved us'; and after preaching and travelling fourscore miles, I was no more tired than when I set out in the morning."

The Pounsetts stayed with Parson Woodforde for some seven weeks. During that time they enjoyed various innocent country diversions, such as catching "a Prodigious fine Pike" weighing eight and a half pounds—with another pike over a pound in weight "in his Belly." They saw off poverty-stricken Cousin Lewis, accompanying him a mile or two on his way, Cousin Lewis who had been staying with Parson Woodforde for a month, having arrived unexpectedly, travelling on foot all the way from Nottinghamshire, with a dog suitably named "Careless." They visited Yarmouth, saw the Cambridge Militia exercising there, and all the flags on the ships flying, it being the King's birthday; moreover, Parson Woodforde bought a fine doll "for Jenny's [his sister's] little maid." They enjoyed a good dinner and an impromptu concert at a neighbouring parson's, ate "vast quantities of Strawberries" after dinner, and thought very handsome "a new silk sack of Lilac colour" worn by a Mrs. Howes.

But now the time when this delightful visit must end was drawing near. On July 6th, 1778, Parson Woodforde accompanied his sister and brother-in-law from Weston Parsonage to Norwich in a chaise; the Parson's mare, on which he was to return home, was led by a servant, and his nephew Bill rode another horse. Two places for the Pounsetts had already been booked on the Norwich–London stage coach by the kind act of a neighbour. At midnight the coach started from the Angel Inn in Norwich Market Place, and Parson Woodforde and his nephew Bill, feeling "rather low" at the parting, saw the Pounsetts off. Then the diarist makes this comment, which lights up in a flash the immense contrast and change between that day and this:

"My poor dear Sister," he says, "shook like an aspin leave going away, she never went in a stage Coach before in her life."

In order to understand Sister Pounsett's feelings, it is necessary to remember certain salient things. In the first

place, the introduction of stage coaches as a normal means
of travel was a relatively recent thing for country dwellers.
Coaches on the few main roads had only become regularly
established since the 1750's or 60's, and those who lived
away from the principal main roads would never see them.
For Sister Pounsett the old-fashioned, familiar method of
travel was riding pillion behind a servant on a horse. And,
in the second place, driving in a stage coach at midnight
had its very real perils, not only because the surface of the
roads was far from perfect, but also because highwaymen
still haunted the wayside. Only three years before, in 1775,
on this very road, the guard of the Norwich stage coach
was killed in Epping Forest, after a fierce fight, in which
he had shot dead three out of the seven highwaymen who
had attacked him in order to rob the mail.

It is odd to think that those friendly and pacific men,
the guards of railway trains, owe their title to their ancestor
of the stage and mail coaches. But so it is, and in the
difference both of duties and of appearance as between the
guard of the coach and the guard of the train, is written
a large page of history. The guard of the coach was heavily
armed with blunderbuss and pistols. It was his duty to
defend the coach from attack by highwaymen, and, after
1784, when the mail coach was introduced, he was specific-
ally the guardian of the mails. As such he was a servant of
the Post Office, clad in a livery of royal scarlet with a gold
band round his hat. It was specially also his duty to see
that the coach kept to its time-table, and that punctually
to the second the various "stages" of the journey were

accomplished. This last duty alone survives for his modern descendant, the railway guard. Only, in place of the horn, which with cheerful note warned the passengers of departure and sometimes was even known to play such sweet songs as "Cherry Ripe," we have now to put up with a shrill and piercing whistle, while blunderbuss, pistols and scarlet coat have disappeared, to be succeeded by the green flag of safety and the dark blue serge of a dull day.

The coaches, which Parson Woodforde and De Quincey, and Charles Dickens, in the person of Mr. Pickwick, had known so well, were swept off the roads between 1830 and 1850. Speed, safety, comfort, convenience, these material advantages of trains conquered the coaches in that twenty years, though the battle was really lost in the first ten. But in two ways trains were, and are, inferior: in the first place, they cannot convey the thrill of the ups and downs and twists of the road, and, in the second place, though steam can be beautiful, as Turner was quick to show, it can never be quite as beautiful as galloping horses. The first named inferiority has now been overcome, not by the trains, but by their rivals the motor-coaches. The road has come into its own again, and something of the old romance of it comes back when a shining monster glides past with Birkenhead or Bath, Oxford or Edinburgh blazoned upon it.

But there never can return, it seems, that divine rapture of the rushing horses, the sharp beauty of jingling harness, of wheels awhirl and glistening, all that happy sense of excitement and adventure which comes but faintly to us now on the dying echoes of a horn.

Chapter Nine

MORNING

There is a verse in the Bible of eleven words—each one a monosyllable—which is all-sufficient. If the literature of the world were to be caught up and burned in a vast bonfire, and if those eleven words alone survived among the ashes, and could be deciphered from the whirling scraps of burned parchment and paper, they would of themselves inspire a new literature.

"And God said, Let there be light: and there was light."

What were the heaven and the earth without light, with only darkness upon the face of the deep? Who could work at all, even God himself, in darkness and obscurity and shadow?

When the Archangel Raphael was telling Adam and Eve about the beginning of all things, he describes how

> *The King of Glory in his powerful Word*
> *And Spirit coming to create new Worlds,*

accompanied by all the hierarchies of heaven, viewed the chaos before Him:

> *the vast immeasurable Abyss*
> *Outrageous as a Sea, dark, wasteful, wilde,*
> *Up from the bottom turn'd by furious windes*
> *And surging waves, as Mountains to assault*
> *Heavens highth, and with the Center mix the Pole.*

185

Milton's profound poetry seems to be describing the modern scene—sound and fury in Spain, fear in Europe, warfare in Abyssinia. We can take hope. All this has happened before—the furious winds and surging waves, dark, wasteful, wild. But then Chaos heard the Voice, and witnessed the creative act of order. And immediately after the firmament had taken form there came the essential sequence, the creation of light.

. . . .

Night has brooded far too long over the entire world. The sun has suffered eclipse since August, 1914. The Armistice brought a dawn so pale that the survivors could hardly see one another. And since then even that light has again receded, so that men have grown bat-like, and flutter about from dark suspicion to dark suspicion, manufacturing nightmares. Nevertheless, the world is on the verge of supreme possibilities of happiness, if only it can gather the imaginative strength to cast away the thought of darkness. Everywhere, if we can but escape from fear and inferiority complexes—everywhere, as never before, is an abundance of good things.

Were Milton's "Omnific Word" to speak in the factories and in the fields and to say, "Put forth now all your strength, produce the fruits of peace," no single soul need know want again in all the world. So enormous have been the strides made by men in their command of the forces of nature. The firmament is there. But it is in darkness and we cannot see.

It is needful to renew the morning habit of mind. And there is no better way of renewal than to stroll with the poets who know more of morning than other men. Listen first in that blissful Garden of Eden to Adam and Eve, just risen from their bower, singing their morning hymn:

> *On Earth joyn all yee Creatures to extoll*
> *Him first, him last, him midst, and without end.*
> *Fairest of Stars, last in the train of Night,*
> *If better thou belong not to the dawn,*
> *Sure pledge of day, that crownst the smiling morn*
> *With thy bright circlet, praise him in thy Spheare*
> *While day arises, that sweet hour of Prime.*

" That sweet hour of Prime!" The very words usher in, are a passport to, faith and hope and peace. And when the hymn was ended the poet says:

> *So prayed they innocent, and to thir thoughts*
> *Firm Peace recoverd soon and wonted calm.*

That certainly was my experience as I read. What a mistake to listen in to Hitler or Mussolini when one might listen in to our first parents!

It was on an early morning close on one hundred and fifty years ago that the youthful Wordsworth received a prophetic intimation of immortality:

> *Magnificent*
> *the morning rose, in memorable pomp,*
> *Glorious as e'er I had beheld—in front,*
> *The sea lay laughing at a distance; near,*
> *The solid mountains shone, bright as the clouds,*
> *Grain-tinctured, drenched in empyrean light;*

187

And in the meadows and the lower grounds
Was all the sweetness of a common dawn—
Dews, vapours, and the melody of birds,
And labourers going forth to till the fields.

It is high time for a disenchanted generation, disenchanted
with its own dust and ashes, to drink deep of the fountains
of pure poetry which have welled up in the ages of faith.
Why not return to Robert Browning?

Thither our path lies; wind we up the heights:
Wait ye the warning?
Our low life was the level's and the night's;
He's for the morning.

Or drop back three centuries to the supreme master of
poetic prose:

"The Pilgrim they laid in a large upper Chamber, whose
window opened towards the Sun rising; the name of the
Chamber was *Peace*, where he slept till break of day; and
then he awoke and sang."

Chapter Ten

EASTER DAY

But Easter Day breaks: But
Christ rises!

Is it the memory of bygone readings of Robert Browning's poem—that sudden dramatic end to all the argument of how hard it is to be a Christian—which makes the magic of these words?

The poet proves the uselessness of anything like a "scientific faith," a contradiction in terms, something not in the least worth having, and guides you down the difficult pathways of his thought, a long and twisting journey, to the sharp revelation at the close. Or is it little to do with the poem, or with Browning, that the words have their power, their virtue consisting in their immemorial associations, the supreme miracle of the Gospels?

In thinking out the answer we recall how other poets have been inspired by the mere thought of Easter: there is the sonnet, lyrical with joy, which Spenser buried like a rich jewel amongst the earthly *Amoretti*:

> *Most glorious Lord of lyfe that on this day,*
> *Didst make thy triumph over death and sin:*
> *And having harrowed hell didst bring away,*
> *Captivity thence captive us to win.*
> *This joyous day, deare Lord, with joy begin.*

Or there is George Herbert's lark-like anthem:

> *Rise, heart, thy Lord is risen; sing His praise*
> *with out delayes;*
>
> . . . .
>
> *Awake, my lute, and struggle for thy part*
> *with all thy art;*
>
> . . . .
>
> *Consort both heart and lute, and twist a song*
> *Pleasant and long.*

No! These are but the bright signals of the central truth. Nor would the poets claim more than that their words, in so far as they are touched with the authentic fire, have caught their glow from the pure flame of the Gospels.

Read again the account of the Resurrection in Matthew, Mark, Luke and John! Never was any story told with such consummate simplicity and economy. Matthew describes the miracle of that early morning in ten verses, Mark in eight, Luke in twelve, John in eighteen. How wearisome seem all the thousand upon thousand volumes of theological exposition in the face of this divine brevity! In so few words —but words each one of which is translucent with beauty and with truth—was revealed the mystery which has been the loftiest hope and inspiration of men for two thousand years!

For evermore is graven into our minds the stupendous experience of Mary Magdalene. To have watched the Crucifixion; to have mourned through the long ceremonious Sabbath when her Redeemer lay in the sepulchre; to have come to that silent Garden where He was buried, as early as she could, when it was still dark, on the first day of the week; to endure the final shock—the stone rolled away and the body gone; so bewildered with weeping that she simply cannot understand what the angels are saying to her, nor recognise Jesus who was standing beside her. At last, when He had called her by her name, the momentous miracle became manifest:

"Jesus saith unto her, Mary! She turned herself, and saith unto him, Rabboni! which is to say, Master!"

Chapter Eleven

THE WISE MEN

It was just after Christmas that they came, the Wise Men, whom after-ages created into kings, bringing their gifts of gold and frankincense and myrrh. And yet one associates them with the shepherds and their flock, the Angel and the multitude of the Heavenly Host, and rightly and naturally with the Star of Bethlehem. The great painters and the great poets are partly responsible for this, the earliest, recollection of childhood, which likes to think that the Child received presents too on His birthday, even though He was so poor as to be born in a stable.

> *See how from far upon the Eastern rode*
> *The Star-led Wizards haste with odours sweet:*
> *O run, prevent them with thy humble ode.*
> *And lay it lowly at his blessed feet.*

So Milton ushers in his Hymn on the Morning of Christ's Nativity; and Perugino adorns a serene fresco of the Adoration of the Kings with a background of sheep and shepherds, green pastures, and a courtly stable, a star shining down in broad daylight, while a long procession headed by the bearers of the gold, frankincense, and myrrh approaches Mary; then they kneel down before the King of Kings and Lord of Lords, the only Ruler of Princes.

After all, only twelve days separate Epiphany from Christmas, and those days mingle together into one great day of Manifestation which was to transform the history of the world. Indeed, the Eastern Church originally combined together, in its ancient Epiphany, events so separate as the Nativity, the Baptism, and the first miracle at Cana. Time stood still. And every year of the nearly 2,000 since then, time stops and stays at Christmas, just as the Star "stood over where the young child was." How well one remembers that night when one was first lifted out of bed and shown the Star of Bethlehem. "Look," said the nurse, "there is the Star!" I looked, and there it was, brilliant in the sky, immense, so it seemed, dwarfing all other stars with its steadfast radiance.

It is said that for four years in succession before the birth of Christ the Dog-star Sirius shone at sunrise upon the first of the month Mesori, which, being interpreted, means "the birth of the prince." With what a wonder must the three Wise Men, of whom we should think as of three eminent members of the Royal Society engaged to-day on some profound research in physical or astronomical science, with what awe must they have observed this extraordinary phenomenon in the heavens! We see them on a hoary mountain in Assyria, or Egypt, or Persia, scanning the sky during those years of prelude, pondering on the meaning of Sirius and his manifestations; finally, struck with the splendour of scientific inspiration, they reach their provisional conclusion. Yes! They will put this poignant and agitating idea to the test. They mount their camels for the

1,000-mile journey over the desert, over the ancient hills, and through the waters of the south. Slowly they wind along—Kaspar, slightly bowed with age, his white beard and hair telling his years; Melchior, in middle life and prime of scientific attainment; and Balthazar, beautiful with the grace of youth and ardour for the revelation of the mystery. What if Sirius had deceived them after all! Three years in succession they have seen him: the fourth is the decisive period: in that year they have set out, and after months of journeying they approach Jerusalem.

They ask of Herod, the King, "Where is he that is born King of the Jews? His Star we have seen where the sun rises, and we have come to cast ourselves in obeisance before him." Herod, small, worldly king, is jealous and alarmed. He calls his Cabinet and asks them where Christ is to be born. They search the archives, and reply in memorable words:

"In Bethlehem of Judea: for thus it is written by the Prophet,
And thou, Bethlehem, in the land of Juda, art not the least among the princes of Juda: for out of thee shall come a Governor, that shall rule my people Israel."

Kaspar, Melchior, and Balthazar looked at one another and nodded. The weariness of their limbs left them. The problem was almost unravelled. They must set on instantly for Bethlehem.

Night had already come down, but they would not wait. To-morrow was the first of the month Mesori, and Sirius would appear at dawn in splendour. The camels quickened their pace, and darkness was no longer darkness to the Wise Men, as they hurried over the last six miles of their pilgrimage.

Dawn was beginning to streak the heavens when they reached the outskirts of Bethlehem. They searched the eastern sky with anxious eyes, and Balthazar could hardly contain his emotion. Even Kaspar and Melchior trembled as they crouched upon their camels. Then Balthazar cried out, and pointed at the first mild beam of shining Sirius. Spellbound, they watched. It seemed that as the beams expanded they shone down with a peculiar brightness and glory on to a shattered stable on the very edge of the city. The Wise Men climbed down from their camels with shaking limbs. They untied the box which Kaspar had carried, containing those regal gifts which were at once the symbols of their faith and the vindication of their science.

They approached the stable, which the Star had now noosed in a circle of serene light. There "they saw the young Child with Mary, his Mother." They fell down and worshipped Him. And as they worshipped, calm came to them. They knew at last what Truth was, and their minds were soothed with a sense of enormous tranquillity. Quietly they opened their treasures, and presented to the Child gold, and frankincense, and myrrh.

Chapter Twelve

CLOTHALL

The church and the small village are perched on the hills, just two miles above Baldock, on the road to Royston and Cambridge. Windmill Hill, Newfield Hill, and Bird Hill are marked on the Ordnance map and slope up from Clothall Common, which, in fact, is not a common, but one of the relatively few remaining unenclosed parts of England, matching Bygrave Common on the other side of the railway. Each of these wide commons is richly cultivated, particularly on the Clothall side, where market gardens are adding to the patterned beauty of the unhedged, wide-stretching fields. The whole area gives the impression of sowing and reaping from time immemorial, and the still remaining "Balks" and "Linces" have been photographed not seldom for standard works on economic history.

With these, however, we are not concerned, save only as they form the physical prelude to the peace of Clothall. No! Not only physical, because the sense of the endless procession of labourers on that quiet land fits in well with the mood in which you climb up to the church, the small hills forming interlacing arcs on either side, with the symmetry of rainbows which forget to end and begin again.

From generation to generation! Time without beginning and without end! With these feelings drifting in from the hot summer fields and the pleasantly winding road among the hills, you reach a sign-post on the right—two miles from Baldock—and turning up this shady way, and advancing 200 or 300 yards, you will come upon a decorous drive leading into the rectory—as it was once—and beside it a footpath pointing uphill to the church.

You walk up the footpath and, as you mount, look across at the rectory, which seems to insist on being seen. An exceedingly pleasant early Georgian house it is, of considerable size and dignity: its red bricks turned just the right colour and its gardens ablaze with roses. Very much as Dr. John Savage intended it should look, for he built it just about 200 years ago. He calls very particular attention to it in the deftly turned Latin epitaph composed by himself for the black marble slab in the chancel, adorned with six savage lions.

For it appears that this Georgian parson, after perambulating almost all Europe, and at length returning and settling down, determined to reconstruct the rectorial buildings on a more august scale—*"in formam augustiorem"*; proceeded also to enlarge and adorn the grounds; finally had it in his mind, if strength had sufficed, to restore the church, "this temple sacred to God." But death unfortunately snatched him. Snatched him, too, in a very odd way, but this the epitaph naturally could not record, as the doctor—he was a Doctor of Divinity of both Universities—had not second sight. It seems he was examining, presumably out of pure curiosity, the scaffold being erected for the execution of the wicked Lord Lovat of the '45 rebellion, when he fell down the scaffold stairs and so died on March 24th, 1747.

A witty man, a good scholar, devoted to his old school, Westminster, from whence he had proceeded to Emmanuel College, Cambridge. But his heart was at Westminster, when it was not at Clothall decorating the rectory. So much so, that the Westminster boys erected a Latin epitaph in white marble to his memory at their own cost on the East Cloister wall of the Abbey, to the right of the door leading into the Chapter House. The song of a boy would not be displeasing, they thought, to one who had been used to play the boy with them, who had ever been mindful of their school, and whom the genius of the place mourned.

On account of his wit he was called the Aristippus of his age. George I rallied him at a levée on the length of his stay in Rome when travelling with his patron, Lord Salisbury: "You stayed long enough; why did you not convert the Pope?" "Because, Sir," replied the incorrigible doctor, "I had nothing better to offer him."

In his younger days, in 1704, Dr. Savage preached a sermon: "Security of the Established Religion the Wisdom of the Nation." With this in mind we can hardly think the doctor would have approved the sale of his beautiful rectory for a private residence, or the combination of the benefice of Clothall with that of Baldock. But, as we know to our cost, necessity knows no law, and the Church suffers with the times. We can only regret that in so many parishes of England the combination policy has been the only means of meeting the difficulty caused by the diminished numbers of the clergy.

Nevertheless, Clothall has not lost, and never will lose, its spiritual identity, so long as its twelfth-century church, with fourteenth-century tower, chancel, and south chapel, stands on its hill looking out over hill and valley, cornfield and pasture.

The long succession of rectors buried in the chancel, including three in Eucharistic vestments, exquisitely cut in brass, Dominus John Vynter, 1404, Cleric John Wright, 1519, sometime Master of Trinity College, Cambridge, and Master Thomas Dalyson, 1541, not least Parson William Lucas, in canonicals, who lived to be ninety-six and died in the five-and-fortieth year of the "reigne of oure soveraigne Lady Queene Elizabeth," insist on Clothall's independent peace. So do the painted birds in the fourteenth-century chancel window, perhaps copied by the medieval artist from those which used to fly over Bird Hill. So do the two little sons of the Caroline poet, Thomas Stanley, whom the Lord gave and took away so soon from the sorrowing parents. Nevertheless, blessed be His name—*sit nomen Domini benedictum.*

But we must begin to turn home, for the summer afternoon is already far gone, and soon over Clothall evening once more, "Nymph reserved," will with her

> *Dewy fingers draw*
> *The gradual dusky veil.*

Chapter Thirteen

BERESFORD DALE

The exquisite picture in *The Times* of Friday, October 28th, 1932, shows that Charles Cotton and Izaak Walton would not have to lament any loss of the old beauty if they were to awake from their seventeenth-century sleep. Old Izaak was wont to say that only "Sir Philip Sidney or Mr. Cotton's father" could describe "the pleasantness of the river, mountains, and meadows" about Beresford Hall, where he used to stay in Beresford Dale with his friend Charles. And as for Charles himself, he doted on the place, so that one wanders about it, in and out of his prose and poetry, as naturally as he did himself. For that is Cotton's distinctive literary achievement, an effortless simplicity of expression which Coleridge, to say nothing of Charles Lamb and Wordsworth, found so pleasing.

Here are *Piscator* and *Viator* in Beresford Dale in the year 1676—Cotton wrote his part of *The Compleat Angler* in ten days there, in the spring of that year:

Piscator: But look you, Sir, now you are abroad, does not the sun shine as bright here as in Essex, Middlesex, or Kent, or any of your Southern countries?

Viator: 'Tis a delicate morning, indeed, and I now think this a marvellous pretty place.

Piscator: . . . But look you, Sir, now you are at the

brink of the hill, how do you like my river; the vale it winds through, like a snake; and the situation of my little fishing-house?

Viator: Trust me, 'tis all very fine. . . .

And here he is writing to a friend, John Bradshaw, in one of those poetical epistles of which he was so fond:

> *My River still through the same channel glides,*
> *Clear from the tumult, salt, and dirt of tides,*
> *And my poor Fishing-House, my seat's best grace,*
> *Stands firm and faithfull in the self-same place;*
> *I left it four months since, and ten to one*
> *I go a fishing ere two days are gone.*

There, in that remote solitude—and was not solitude, after all, "the soul's best friend"—Cotton could escape finally from the world, could even hide himself, in the cave in the river's precipitous bank, from those intolerable bailiffs who were perpetually dunning him for the money which somehow slipped through his fingers so fast.

It was his father, Charles Cotton the elder, who had begun the process of mortgaging and selling, and the son brought the practice to its inevitable end. The broad acres there, in the Dale, and over the Derbyshire border, had fallen into the elder Cotton's lap by the simple process of an elopement. Olivia Beresford, whom Michael Drayton mourned in an elegy, the heiress of it all, had married Sir John Stanhope, and their only child Olive, before she was sixteen—it was rather like Romeo and Juliet—found Charles Cotton irresistible. It was not surprising. Even the sober

Lord Clarendon, Lord Chancellor of England and eminent historian, wrote about the elder Charles Cotton in his autobiography with a hand which trembled a little as he thought back into the youthful years of friendship:

"He had all those qualities which in youth raise men to the reputation of being fine gentlemen: such a pleasantness and gaiety of humour, such a sweetness and gentleness of nature, and such a civility and delightfulness in conversation, that no man, in the Court or out of it, appeared a more accomplished person; all these extraordinary qualifications being supported by as extraordinary a clearness of courage and fearlessness of spirit, of which he gave too often manifestation."

This charming person, having successfully eloped with Olive, tried to placate her angry father, Sir John Stanhope, by protesting "the passion and fervency of affection," which had transported him possibly beyond the bounds of wisdom in the affair. Sir John could only splutter out "perjury, unlawful practices, conspiracies, riots, riotous assemblies." But it was too late. The result of the passion and fervency was Charles Cotton the younger, who was born in April 1630, and was to justify it all by writing Part II of *The Compleat Angler*, some exquisite love lyrics and poems of Nature, by translating Montaigne's *Essays* into limpid English, and by numerous other literary excursions carried out in the seclusion of his valley, with the Dove murmuring by.

For he lived most of his life in Beresford Dale, apart from a visit to France during the period of the Protectorate and a brief jaunt to Ireland later on. He married, very happily, his cousin, Isabella Hutchinson, daughter of Sir Thomas and a half-sister of the famous Colonel Hutchinson, and they had nine children, of whom five survived.

Thy Summer's bower shall overlook
The subtle windings of the brook.

So he sang to Isabella, and went out and fished and shot hares:

At the first peep of day I'll rise
To make the sullen hare thy prize,
And thou with open arms shalt come
To bid thy hunter welcome home.

His extravagance, or inability to control the opening of his purse with so large a family to maintain, perhaps caused Isabella anxiety; but she was spared the final wrench, for she died in April 1669, before her husband was compelled to sell Beresford Hall. This happened in 1681, and the property was bought by his cousin, John Beresford. Six years later, in London, the poet died and was buried in St. James's, Piccadilly.

Sometimes I have sought him there, escaping into that oasis of peace in the midst of the roar of traffic. But I have not found him. And I know now why it is. He has returned to Beresford Dale. There, very early in the morning, you may see him, walking with Izaak Walton, ghostly rods in their hands, beside the silver Dove. "Simon Peter said, I go a fishing: and they said, We also will go with thee."

Chapter Fourteen

REFLECTIONS ON BACON

It is not the purpose of this essay to add anything to the windy Baconian–Shakespeare controversy, nor to defend nor attack the character of the great Lord Chancellor, but simply to discourse of Bacon, and more plainly of pigs. Nevertheless, as the name of Lord Bacon has been mentioned I would have the reader realise that the crest of that great lord, descended from an honourable family of Suffolk country gentlemen, was simply a pig, or, as heraldry prefers to designate it, a boar. Thus, in the description of the Bacon pedigree you will read: "*Crest*, on a wreath Argent and Gules, a boar passant Ermine."

It pleases me to think that one of the wisest men who ever lived was named Bacon, and connected his name with the animal which provides that fragrant and essential article of diet. The whole tribe of pigs, I feel, is ennobled by such a connection, and as they have been constantly vilified they can grunt out this retort for the future. Natural philosophers among the animals, regarding truth as an eternal trough which never satisfies the appetite, and meditative slumber as one of the supreme gifts and joys of life, their name, or the name of their flesh, has been honoured, not only in the person of the supreme essayist, but in the person of an Oxford scholar, one of the early fathers of medieval-modern

205

philosophy, Roger Bacon, monk of the Order of St. Francis, and inventor, alas! of gunpowder.

But widespread as is the family and name of Bacon among men, the marvel is that we are not all, or almost all, Bacons, though we could not expect all to be philosophers. For in ancestral times, times before and since the Norman Conquest, England was a perfect paradise of pigs, and the number of swineherds must have been enormous. In the great inventory which the Conqueror caused to be composed of the wealth of his new realm, one of the entries which you hardly ever fail to find is the calculation of the amount of sustenance in the manor for our immemorial friends. "Wood" or, as some prefer to call it, "pannage" for a thousand pigs (*porcis* or *porcorum* as the Norman scribe penned it), for four hundred and fifty pigs, for two hundred pigs, for one hundred pigs: there it all is in minute detail. So that one of the most distinctive sounds in the woody purlieus of the villages and townships of England must have been a deep, contemplative, philosophising grunt, interspersed now and again by a sharp and piercing squeal and rushing sound of heavy bodies disappearing among the trees, as the traveller from afar startled and disturbed the placid porkers.

Why have pigs been so notoriously abused? I turn up my Little Oxford Dictionary, indispensable companion, under *pig*: I read "swine, hog; person like pig in greed, dirt, or perversity." I look up *swine*, and after being told that the word means "kinds of non-ruminant carnivorous[1] animal,"

[1] Is this a slip for *omnivorous*?

am also informed that it can stand for a "bestial or degraded person, lover of filth." After this one can hardly bear to look up *hog*.

With my present passion for pigs I find it melancholy to think that naughty children in the nursery call one another "greedy pigs," or "horrid little pigs," or that naughtier men refer to one another, on occasion, as "swine" or as "bestial hogs." Nor can I escape from this grave slander on the pig race when I seek relief in literature:

> *To roll with pleasure in a sensual sty,*

I read in *Comus*, or again:

> *for swinish gluttony*
> *Ne'er looks to Heaven amidst his gorgeous feast,*
> *But, with besotted base ingratitude,*
> *Crams, and blasphemes his Feeder.*

Now, as for dirt, pigs are really very clean creatures if given proper accommodation and some decent straw. As for greed, certainly not even the most sincere apologist of pigs or lover of bacon can deny that they enjoy their victuals. But reflect, reader, how it would be with you if you had an immensely long, barrel-shaped and capacious body carried on four very short legs: if you had a nose (or snout), especially constructed and designed to go to the root of matters: if you had a mouth of peculiar capacity, stretching almost from ear to ear. (And, by the way, what charming ears, too, eminently adapted for flapping and, at the same time, for composing the eye for slumber beneath their ample shade!)

Would you not enjoy your food even more than you do now? Would you not grunt, and even slightly squeal, with the excruciating ecstasy of creamy, rich barley-meal, as it entered your long and wide mouth, gurgled in your roomy throat and flowed on into that vast stomach for ever clamouring to be soothed?

Think, too, reader, that all this eagerness for sustenance is for you; that this anxiety, mis-named greed, is essentially vicarious; that, in short, these pigs are, with an extra-ordinary diligence, hastening to the supreme end of things in all its rich variety of pork, of sausages, of souse, of chine and cheek, and flitch of bacon! I will not go so far as to say with Cobbett, that "a couple of flitches of bacon are worth fifty thousand Methodist sermons and religious tracts": Cobbett had his knife into the Methodists as he had into many other wholly excellent people, and no attention should be paid to his ridiculous diatribes save in the way of pleasant laughter. But I agree with him that

"the sight of flitches upon the rack tends more to keep a man from poaching and stealing than whole volumes of penal statutes. . . . They are great softeners of the temper, and promoters of domestic harmony. They are a great blessing. . . ."

Who will not echo the sentiments of old Cobbett, when he recalls that exquisite scent slowly ascending the stairs in the early morning as one comes down to breakfast, or hears the sweet sound of sizzling, or sees the curling rashers dancing in the frying-pan? And when is England, ancestral home of generous, philosophic, peaceful pigs, more truly England, than when you step off the boat at Southampton early in the morning, on your return from France, where they understand bacon so little as to call it *lard*, when, I say, you step off the boat and board the train, and entering the restaurant-car, see imprinted upon the menu those spell-binding words:

Eggs and Bacon;

Tomatoes and Bacon;

Bacon . . . ?

Chapter Fifteen

OLD THAMES

In the *Globe Encyclopædia*, published in 1879, in the article on London, you may read the following, among many proud boasts of the capital's greatness: "For the conveyance of the inhabitants, besides private carriages, 8,000 cabs and 1,500 omnibuses are in constant use. Hundreds of little steamers ply continually on the river." Cabs—taxi-cabs—omnibuses and trams have since then immensely multiplied. And the steamers—what of them?

The question can receive but an unsatisfactory and melancholy answer. Where, about half a century ago, hundreds were continually plying, one may to-day see an occasional steamer with trippers, or a motor-boat with some river police. It would be almost incredible, if it were not too plain a fact, that at a time when the streets of London are intolerably congested by traffic, and the trains and tubes are filled to suffocation, the noblest highway in London is deserted. Surely it is high time for Londoners to wake up and realise their loss, not only in material convenience, but in the amenities of life!

Who, living, say, at Hammersmith, Chiswick, Kew or Richmond, would stagger up the stairs of an omnibus, or sway in the train upon a strap, if he might take a seat in a comfortable motor-launch and accomplish his journey in beauty and peace? It may be that the day of large steamers has gone by: if so, has not the day of the lesser motor-launch arrived?

It is not, however, my purpose here to suggest the precise methods whereby river traffic should be revived. That is a question which must be solved by intelligent private enterprise.

Let me rather open some windows into the past, and ask the reader to look through them. After all, loss must be realised before it can be made good. The present generation has never really known the Thames. The older generation, our great-grandfathers and our great-great-grandfathers, must speak, and explain to their descendants how much they have missed, and are missing.

Let us go back first no further than the reign of Charles II. Count Grammont, in his *Memoirs*, has left an unforgettable description of those "shows" on the river in the 1660's, which he said only the City of London could afford to the sightseer. He is describing the river as it flowed past the Palace of Whitehall—the Palace survives to-day only in the exquisite Banqueting Hall, now the United Services Museum, and in some internal portions of the Treasury—and how from the river-stairs of the Palace the Court used to embark to take the air on stifling summer days:

"An infinite Number of open Boats, full of the celebrated Beauties of the Court and City, attended the Barges in which were the Royal Family: And Collations, Musick, and Fireworks compleated the Entertainment. The Chevalier

[Grammont himself] always made one of the Company; and generally added something of his own Invention, to heighten the Diversion by some surprising Stroke of Magnificence and Gallantry. Sometimes, he had compleat Consorts of Voices and Instruments, which he privately sent for from Paris, and which struck up, on a sudden, in those courtly Cruizes."

Pepys estimated that on August 23rd, 1662, ten thousand boats and barges welcomed Catherine of Braganza when, as the Bride of Charles II, she made her royal entry into London, voyaging under a canopied barge from Hampton Court. His *Diary* is filled almost daily with accounts of river journeys—when boats and barges occupied the place of our taxis and 'buses. In almost the last entry, the entry for May 28th, 1669 (the *Diary* ends on May 31st), he tells how he and his wife and brother:

"Spent the evening on the water, carrying our supper with us, as high as Chelsea; so home, making sport with the Westerne bargees, and my wife and I singing, to my great content."

It would probably be undesirable, even if it were possible, to put the clock back; but wise progress partly depends on, and consists in, conserving the best elements of the passing years, and there is clearly no reason why Londoners, even if they must endure the deafening roar of modern road traffic, should not soothe their nerves by hearing music where, mysteriously, it sounds best—upon the water.

Throughout the eighteenth century the citizens of London

well appreciated the use and beauty of their river; and not only the citizens. Parson Woodforde, just after his election to a Fellowship at New College, Oxford, on July 22nd, 1761, took a jaunt with three friends to London. They started by coach from Oxford at five o'clock in the morning and reached Hyde Park Corner at tea-time. They then proceeded to the river, embarked in a boat, and visited the gaieties of Vauxhall, that permanent eighteenth-century equivalent of our fleeting Earl's Court Exhibitions, White Cities and Wembleys.

Those who have followed with rapt interest the career and escapades of the agreeable William Hickey will recall how much of the innocent portion of a not very innocent youth was spent on the river. How he kept his boat at Roberts' at Lambeth, what charming expeditions he went with the rich and benevolent Mr. Smith of Battersea— especially that delightful trip of April 20th to May 2nd, 1768, on the *Lovely Mary*, a rather heavy sailer, but "with capital accommodation, having a spacious cabin aft her whole width with sash windows astern." Then there was that unparalleled rowing feat of June 1768, in the rowing cutter for eight persons, "in which we made excursions on the Thames; wore very smart uniforms, having a waterman in a rich livery to steer us." On that particular occasion they rowed from Lambeth, starting at 4.0 a.m., to Gravesend; then back past Lambeth to Richmond. At Richmond they rested four hours and then returned to Lambeth by 10.30 p.m., "having thus rowed ourselves full 130 miles in 13 hours." In 1773 we learn that rowing ceased to be the

214

fashion for smart young men, being supplanted by sailing. Of course, Hickey got a small yacht, formed a sailing club with other sparks, and dined weekly at the Swan Tavern at Chelsea.

It is not necessary to dwell further on the delights of the Thames anywhere between Lambeth and London Bridge in the eighteenth century. If, however, any reader suffers from a sluggish imagination, or may be inclined to scepticism, he should turn over some eighteenth-century prints; there is a pleasant collection of Thames views in the Print Portfolios in the London Library. There he will see the Thames against a background of church spires, and pleasant houses directly overlooking the river, with frequent landing-stages and attractive steps. The river itself is speckled with numberless craft: watermen's rowing boats crowd around the steps; charming yachts puff their sails; commercial barges lumber along with merchandise, and State barges are propelled by gallant-looking oarsmen.

A century or so passes, and we gaze again at the Thames— say, from Westminster Bridge. True, the Embankment is magnificent, and the new London County Council Office has a terrace which looks as though it were meant as a landing-stage for gay and crowded boats. Yes, there is actually a steamer at the Westminster Pier embarking sightseers for Hampton Court or Greenwich, and a motor-launch or two in the offing. But where are "the hundreds of steamers" we heard about as continually plying as late as 1879? And why did the pageant of the Lord Mayor's annual visit in gorgeous barge to Westminster, accompanied by the princely barges of the City Companies, cease in 1856? And why, in the name of common sense and sanity, is the Thames no longer alive with vessels relieving the indecent congestion of railway, tram and 'bus? The great river is silent, and glides imperturbably by. Perhaps it reflects on its past glories, and laments the indifference and insensibility of the myriad citizens of modern London. For it is not difficult to imagine that this nobly moving stream is animate, and sings to itself a song. Many poets have sung to it, and this essay may fitly end with the concluding lines of Crabbe's *Village*, written in 1783:

> *Or as old Thames, borne down with decent pride,*
> *Sees his young streams run warbling at his side;*
> *Though some, by art cut off, no longer run,*
> *And some are lost beneath the summer's sun—*
> *Yet the pure stream moves on, and, as it moves,*
> *Its power increases and its use improves;*
> *While plenty round its spacious waves bestow,*
> *Still it flows on, and shall for ever flow.*

Chapter Sixteen

SUPPING WITH THE POETS

When Bolingbroke had been sentenced to banishment by King Richard II, Shakespeare closes that long scene with a stately farewell between father and son. Old John of Gaunt urges Bolingbroke to look upon his banishment as a kind of blessing, to treat necessity as a virtue; Bolingbroke retorts in impassioned rhetoric:

> *Oh! who can hold a fire in his hand*
> *By thinking on the frosty Caucasus?*
> *Or cloy the hungry edge of appetite*
> *By bare imagination of a feast?*
> *Or wallow naked in December snow*
> *By thinking on fantastic summer's heat?*

I confess that I have never tried any of these experiments in a literal sense, and for present purposes let us forget about holding a fire in the hand, or wallowing naked in December snow. But the second experiment is less painful to contemplate, and for my part—though it does not answer Bolingbroke completely—I make so bold as to aver that no feast of City Company, on the one hand, nor of exquisite privacy, on the other, has ever given me the consummate thrill which I constantly and instantly receive when supping with the poets.

Now it is an odd thing, but nevertheless true—until this statement is controverted in the next issue of the *Spectator* by a host of angry experts—that you cannot enjoy an absolutely first-class feast with Shakespeare himself. Certainly there is Falstaff and any quantity of sack, and admirable venison in the Forest of Arden; nor do I forget Justice Shallow's pippins, for I shall return to them anon; but where is the loaded table with every variety of meat and sweet and winking wine which one might have expected with considerable frequency in those rich Tudor times? Had Shakespeare a soul above food? An absurd notion, a question asked only to be answered with a guffaw of negatives. The truth is that Shakespeare, being the supreme artist, provides all the hospitality by mere suggestion, so that you think you have dined eminently in Elizabethan England and elsewhere, while, in fact, it has simply been—to use his own phrase—by bare imagination of a feast!

By this time the reader may be getting hungry, so we had better allay the pangs of hunger by a very choice supper with Keats, which even your squeamish vegetarian —yes! even your "food reformer"—for so the tribe name themselves—can share. Shelley, by the way, is, as Matthew Arnold said in another connection, a beautiful but ineffectual angel for our purpose.

This refreshment has the additional advantage of being in a very pleasant place, no other indeed than Madeline's chamber, "silken, hush'd and chaste," and Porphyro—ah, who would not be waited on by Porphyro!—draws silently from the closet a heap

Of candied apple, quince, and plum, and gourd;
With jellies soother than the creamy curd,
And lucent syrops, tinct with cinnamon;
Manna and dates, in argosy transferr'd
From Fez; and spiced dainties, every one,
*   From silken Samarcand to cedar'd Lebanon.*

These delicates he heaped with glowing hand
On golden dishes and in baskets bright
Of wreathed silver: sumptuous they stand
In the retired quiet of the night,
Filling the chilly room with perfume light.

Do you find that supper, reader, almost too ambrosial, fragrant and delicious? Exciting rather than satisfying the appetite? Well, then! Fly back near a century, to the year 1729 as near as may be, and let us look in at James Thomson; since he will provide us with solid eighteenth century of the very best, in a most pleasant country house in autumn, with the huntsmen just back from the chase and appropriately hungry:

But first the fuel'd chimney blazes wide;
The tankards foam; and the strong table groans
Beneath the smoking Sirloin, stretch'd immense
From side to side; in which, with desperate knife,
They deep incision make, and talk the while
Of England's glory, ne'er to be defac'd,
While hence they borrow vigour: or amain
Into the Pasty plung'd, at intervals,
If stomach keen can intervals allow,
Relating all the glories of the chase.

And for drink, sir! James will fetch you the mighty Punch Bowl "swell'd high with fiery juice," and next the brown October drawn "mature and perfect from his dark retreat of thirty years"; and then, if you wish, you can stay on for "serious drinking," and—James is a trifle vulgar at times —"the table floating round"—you can "swim in mutual swill."

For my part, though no vegetarian or fruitarian, I have always enjoyed more almost than any other that lovely meal which Eve prepared in Paradise for the Archangel Raphael. It is less sumptuous, or perhaps less sensuous, than Porphyro's for Madeline, but sumptuosity is not everything, and Milton, after all, is a greater poetic chef than Keats. In the Fifth Book of *Paradise Lost*, as the reader will perhaps recall, Raphael is sent down to Paradise to warn Adam and Eve of the danger lurking in the garden. Raphael alights on the eastern cliff of Paradise, and moves through the forest towards Adam's bower. Adam catches sight of his winged visitor, lovely as the morn, "skirted his loins and thighs with downy gold and colours dipt in Heav'n." At once he sends Eve to bring the choicest fruits in abundance for their angelic guest, and Eve, "on hospitable thoughts intent," hastens away. She chooses the various fruits with extraordinary care so as to bring "taste after taste upheld with kindliest change." Fruits of all kinds she gathers, for the kinds of all the earth grow in Paradise, whether from India east or west, or Pontus or the Punic coast, "rough, or smooth rin'd, or bearded husk, or shell"; she crushes the grape for drink and "meathes from many a berry, and from sweet kernels prest she tempers dulcet creams." The ground of the bower she strews with rose and "odours from the shrub unfumed." The table was of grassy turf and round it seats of moss: Adam and Raphael fell to their viands with keen hunger, Raphael unhindered by his angelic nature, and Eve

> *Minister'd naked, and their flowing cups*
> *With pleasant liquors crown'd. O innocence*
> *Deserving Paradise! If ever, then,*
> *Then had the Sons of God excuse to have been*
> *Enamour'd at that sight; but in those hearts*
> *Love unlibidinous reign'd, nor jealousy*
> *Was understood, the injured Lover's Hell.*

Is that not a spell-binding meal, melting the heart and calling the lapsed soul back into heavenly places? No one but the supreme magician of melodious verse could so transubstantiate the human into the divine, so that you sit down with Adam and rise with Raphael.

And, when he wishes, Milton can provide a supper wholly of the earth, such as the Devil prepared for temptation of Jesus in the wilderness, as you will find in the Second Book of *Paradise Regained*. But from that we will abstain.

I had wished to refresh myself—so greedy am I of these poetic feasts—with a mountain meal provided by William Wordsworth. But time presses, and all good things come to an end. Only, if you are up that way, call on the Solitary (in the Second Book of the *Excursion*) and try the butter.

And I promised, earlier in the day, to look in on Justice

Shallow again. We must keep that promise; no one but a fool would miss a light supper with Shakespeare, for the treat is rare indeed. "Nay, you shall see my orchard, where, in an arbour, we will eat a last year's pippin of my own graffing, with a dish of caraways, and so forth; come, cousin Silence; and then to bed."

Chapter Seventeen

THROCKING

I do not know what took me there first unless it was the name, or it may have been the mural painting of St. Christopher close by at Cottered, so that after gazing at the huge legs of Christopher crossing the river, an odd background of fourteenth or fifteenth-century houses being on either side, one was beckoned on to Throcking, down one of those irresistible, winding country roads. It was in autumn, and, as it seemed, out of a reaped cornfield rose the church, guarded, however, from the reaper by a ring of trees, elms, chestnuts and yews.

It is the merit of Gray's *Elegy* that, in its serene stanzas, the poet has described for evermore all English country churches and churchyards, so that if the flood came again and our island world were overwhelmed beneath the waters, the inhabitants of such parts of the earth as survived would, through the printed word, understand something of the ancient peace of England.

Only something, however, for I exaggerate in claiming that the *Elegy* describes all country churches; it would have been truer to say that Gray describes the type and conveys the atmosphere. For each one of the ten thousand English country churches is essentially original and has its own immemorial being, and its own compelling calm.

Throcking, for instance, at once summons the passing traveller to pause: it lies, by the way, not forty miles from London, some two miles from Buntingford in Hertfordshire, and about the same distance to the left of the great Ermine Street as you motor towards Cambridge.

The churchyard is unusually large, and unusually green, and little occupied even by grass-covered graves. An ancient yew tree stretches its consoling arms close by the tower, which itself begins in the thirteenth century and ends with old rose-red bricks, pleasant effort of a seventeenth-century restorer who lies buried in the chancel, with his wife and three sons, "in certaine hope of a joyful resurrection." This was Sir Thomas Soame, Knight, who died in 1670 after an honourable life, Sheriff of the City of London in 1635, and Member of Parliament in the restless years preceding the outbreak of the Civil War. He was on the Royalist side, and perhaps restored the tower of Throcking in gratitude for the restoration of his Prince; for the rebuilding dates, they say, from the year 1660. He died at the ripe age of eighty-eight, having spanned with his father, Sir Stephen Soame, Lord Mayor of London in Queen Elizabeth's reign, near a century and a half. Three daughters of Sir Thomas—Anne, Elizabeth and Mary, tranquil trilogy of names, married and have, I trust, raised up some Soame seed under other surnames.

But the principal monuments in the church are those of the Elwes family, who owned the manor during the whole of the eighteenth century, and commissioned two of the most eminent sculptors of the age to commemorate them.

It must be almost unique to find in so small a church—its whole length of early fifteenth-century nave and chancel is fifty feet—a monument sculptured by Michael Rysbrack on the north wall, and another by Nollekens on the south wall of the nave. Both monuments, it must be admitted, are far too large for the church: they would more appropriately have adorned the transepts of a cathedral. But the sculptors were doubtless well paid by the rich Elwes family—a collateral branch produced the amazing miser, John Elwes, whom Mr. Boffin so admired—and carved and chipped away till great expanses of marble and alabaster enshrined the memories of the dead.

Rysbrack, whose work was completed in 1753, commemorates one Robert Elwes, who is described as "Lord of this Manor and of other Manors in the Counties of Lincoln and York." The inscription further explains that the vault where rest the bones of Robert and his wife has been "by law appropriated for their interment only, exclusive of all others."

Gazing at this vast piece of marble, heavy with plinth and pediment and entablature, surmounted by a large urn and supported by the pomp of heraldic blazonry, you inevitably recall:

> Can storied urn or animated bust
> > Back to its mansion call the fleeting breath?
> Can Honour's voice provoke the silent dust,
> > Or Flattery soothe the dull cold ear of Death?

Nollekens, on the other hand, working in pure alabaster

PP

against a background of grey marble, has produced an exquisite memorial of Hester Elwes, the wife of Cary Elwes, who caused the monument to be erected to his beloved wife.

Here is the eighteenth century in the perfection of its austere interpretation of plastic art, its many-syllabled, grandiloquent prose, its poignant and solemn emotion. Hester Elwes is resting on a seat dressed in a white gown of loosely flowing linen; her head is resting on her left hand, and in her right she holds an open book which she reads with deep attention. Immediately in front of her is the invariable symbol of eighteenth-century mortality, a funeral urn.

The long epitaph below, after recording that she died at the age of forty-seven, on January 14th, 1770, proceeds in an almost impassioned encomium of her life and virtues as follows:

> *In the elegance of her figure, in the sweetness*
> *and civility of her manners, in the excellence*
> *and improvement of her mind and understanding,*
> *   she excelled the generality of her sex;*
> *Nor was she less distinguished for her extensive*
> *   liberality and charity.*
> *Her faith in God, founded alone on the merits of her*
> *   Redeemer, was firm and unshaken;*
> *she met her Dissolution with equal fortitude and*
> *   resignation;*
> *and died full of the hope of a blessed immortality;*
> *to this, the best of wives and parents, as also to*
> *   Robert Cary,*

his amiable son, cut off at a tender age; to Martha,
his beloved daughter, snatched from the breast of her
uniformly tender mother,
     Cary Elwes, Esq., Lord of this Manor,
    her affectionate husband near twenty-eight years,
    erected this monument.

Beneath the epitaph are the Elwes arms, with due quarterings, surmounted by the crest, a writhing serpent transfixed by a sheaf of five feathered arrows, the whole in the lovely brightness of heraldic colour, Or, Argent, Azure and the rest.

It is time to leave Throcking Church, observing that it has somehow subdued the ample marble memorials so as to be not wholly out of accord with its own ultimate simplicity, its very name hardly changed from the plain Trochinge of *Domesday Book*. And so with a backward glance at some little seventeenth-century angels, carved in oak and pretending to support the roof on their wings, we step into the sunlight, pass under the yew, then through a wicket gate into the road, back to the everyday world again.

Chapter Eighteen

JOHN BUNYAN AND WOMEN

"And in this I admire the wisdom of God, that he made me shy of women from my first conversion till now." So Bunyan wrote in his memorable autobiography, whose very title rings like a chime of sweet bells—*Grace Abounding to the Chief of Sinners; or, a brief relation of the exceeding mercy of God in Christ, to his poor servant, John Bunyan.*

Perhaps, because he was shy of women, he was able the better to understand them, like an artist who steps back from his portrait in order to criticise, and make perfect with some finishing strokes of the brush. At any rate it is clear that he had a peculiar reverence for women, which is revealed in his works, the chief of which contains the supreme praise spoken by Gaius, the Innkeeper, who was a Lover of Pilgrims.

If you compare the weaknesses and wickednesses personified in the two parts of *The Pilgrim's Progress* you will find very few assigned to women. True, there is Wanton who promised Faithful all carnal content, so that he had to shut his eyes to save himself from bewitchment: we meet her again in the second part as Madame Wanton in company with Mrs. Light-Mind, Mrs. Love-the-Flesh, and Mrs. Filth. Then there is my Lady Faining, Mrs. Know-Nothing, Mrs. Bats-Eyes, Mrs. Bub.. 'rs. Inconsiderate, Mrs.

Diffidence and Mrs. Timorous. But what are they compared
with the men—Mr. By-Ends, Lord Carnal-Delight, Lord
Old-man, Lord Luxurious, Lord Desire of Vain Glory,
my old Lord Lechery, Sir Having Greedy, Mr. Cruelty,
Messrs. Discontent, Pride, Arrogancy, Self-Conceit, Worldly
Glory, Giant Despair, Lord Fairspeech, Mr. Fearing, Mr.
Feeble-Mind, Mr. Formalist, Mr. Hypocrisy, Lord Hate-
Good, Mr. Hate-Light, Mr. Heady, Mr. Hold-the-World,
Mr. Ignorance, Mr. Implacable, Mr. Linger-after-Lust, Mr.
Liar, Mr. Money-Love? But this is only half-way through
the alphabet and the list is long.

The cynical may say that Bunyan's shyness prevented
him from knowing women as well as he knew men, so that
women's weaknesses escaped his vivid eye. There may be
something in this, but I think the real truth is that he owed
more to women than he owed to men and that he realised
that they had a greater intuitive understanding of religion.
On the other hand it is certainly true that in the rôle of
the positive virtues there are more men than women, which
to some extent helps to balance the scales. And yet I think
Mercy outweighs them all.

Certainly his debt to women was great. It was a woman
who first brought him to his senses over his inordinate
swearing and cursing, so that he was silenced and put to
shame, and from that time forward began to give it up.
After that, when he was passing through his rather smug
phase, he was shown by some poor women what religion
really meant. It was in one of the streets of Bedford that
he overheard these women "sitting at a door in the sun,

and talking about the things of God," and how He had visited their souls with His love. And here one's mind wanders to

> *The spinsters and the knitters in the sun,*
> *And the free maids that weave their thread with bones,*

who sang that song in Shakespeare which "dallies with the innocence of love." And one regrets the self-conscious, conventional age in which we live, so that one neither hears nor sees such pleasant things any longer.

He was evidently singularly happy in both his marriages. His first wife brought him as her dowry two books—she had nothing else, and they were so poor that they had not "a dish or spoon betwixt them both"—*The Plain Man's Pathway to Heaven* and *The Practice of Piety*, which had belonged to her father. In these books he found things pleasing to him. It must have been partly due to her sympathy, we suspect, that his mind did not absolutely give way under those terrible spiritual tortures through which he passed before the grace abounding flowed into his consciousness. He certainly discussed things with her, for there is a passage in that astounding autobiography which in a flash of light shows them talking together in their cottage. He had been very low and ill and was sitting by the fire, when suddenly some words sounded in his heart, very simple words, just: "I must go to Jesus." His darkness and infidelity fled away at these words. But he was astonished and could not, on the spur of the moment, connect them with the Bible. So he turned to his wife. "Wife, said I, is there ever such a scripture, I must go to Jesus?" She, good soul, could not tell. Nevertheless it must have helped him to ask her. And soon other words "came bolting in" upon him: those lovely words: "and to an innumerable company of angels," and then the whole passage in the Epistle to the Hebrews was set before his eyes.

How his second wife pleaded for him before the judges he has himself recorded in an account which he took down from her own mouth, an account of a court scene in 1661 worth numberless volumes of reconstructed history:

Judge Hall: What is his calling?

Answer: Then some of the company that stood by said, A tinker, my Lord.

Woman: Yes, said she, and because he is a tinker, and a poor man, therefore he is despised, and cannot have justice.

This was not quite true, because the judges were only acting under the law; but it was a law contrary to the divine law, was not many years afterwards abrogated, and we love her for saying what she said.

Now when we remember these things we can understand why Bunyan put that superb passage about women into the mouth of Innkeeper Gaius, when he had welcomed Greatheart and old Honest, Christiana and her children, and the Maid Mercy into his comfortable rooms:

"I will say again, that when the Saviour was come, Women rejoyced in him, before either Man or Angel. I read not that ever any man did give unto Christ so much as one Groat, but the Women followed him, and ministered to him of their Substance. 'Twas a Woman that washed his Feet with Tears, and a Woman that annointed his Body to the Burial. They were Women that wept, when he was going to the Cross; and Women that followed him from the Cross, and that sat by his Sepulchre when he was buried. They were Women that was first with him at his Resurrection-morn, and Women that brought Tiding first to his Disciples that he was risen from the Dead."

Not any progress to Calvary, nor descent from the Cross, nor visitation of the tomb, whether painted by a Raphael, Perugino or Michelangelo, can equal this tinker's master-piece of words, instinct with passion and purity and love:

"They were Women that wept, when he was going to the Cross."

No wonder that such divine painting, so solemn a music, such simple succession of words sounding all the depths of prose and of poetry, should have been translated into almost every language under heaven![1]

[1] *The Pilgrim's Progress* has been translated into some hundred and twenty languages and dialects—see the tercentenary edition of Dr. Brown's definitive *Life of Bunyan*, ch. xix and app. ii.

Chapter Nineteen

THE POET GRAY AND PARSON ETOUGH

In a "Sketch of his own Character," Gray wrote that he "could love and could hate, so was thought somewhat odd." Of the warmth of Gray's affection for his friends his letters bear full witness. His letters also show that, like the rest of the world, he had his prejudices and dislikes. But did he actually hate anyone? I think the answer is that one person at least he hated. That person was the Rev. Henry Etough, rector of the valuable living of Therfield, in Hertfordshire, a village some eighteen miles from Cambridge.

In a letter to Horace Walpole, written in 1748, Gray refers to Etough as "a Fiend of a Parson." In another letter to Walpole, dated November 26th, 1751, Gray says a great deal more, as the reader will see if he refers to Vol. II, pp. 118–19, of Dr. Paget Toynbee's *Correspondence of Gray, Walpole, West and Ashton (1734–1771)*. This letter in particular shows how bitterly Gray felt about Parson Etough, how he hated him, and even feared him. He speaks of him almost as one would speak of a cobra lurking in one's kitchen garden. It is, however, unnecessary to search the letters for proof of Gray's feelings, for there exists that scorching epigram which he wrote beneath the etching of the Rev. Henry Etough, made by Gray's Cambridge friend,

Mr. Tyson of Corpus. The picture certainly causes a shiver (it is reproduced in the Oxford edition of Gray's *Poems*, edited in 1917 by Mr. Austin Lane Poole): you would undoubtedly have dived down one of the numberless Cambridge side-lanes had you seen Etough approaching from the direction of the Trumpington road; for he liked Cambridge, and often journeyed there from Therfield.

It is difficult to say if the picture is really a fair likeness,[1] for this Hertfordshire parson was presumably not a *persona grata* with the artist; still it looks uncannily alive. And Gray's lines also are vivid with a sort of shuddering hatred:

> *Thus* Tophet *look'd; so grinned the brawling fiend,*
> *While frighted prelates bow'd, and called him friend;*
> *I saw them bow, and while they wished him dead,*
> *With servile simper nod the mitred head.*
> *Our Mother Church, with half averted sight,*
> *Blush'd as she bless'd her griesly proselyte:*
> *Hosannas rung thro' Hell's tremendous borders,*
> *And Satan's self had thoughts of taking orders.*

Some considerable time after reading Gray's epigram I happened to be turning over the pages of Clutterbuck's magnificent *History of Hertfordshire*, published in three vast folio volumes a century ago. In the third volume is an account of the parishes in the Hundred of Odsey, and in due course comes Therfield, with its interesting manorial and clerical history; for since Henry VIII's time the parish has been closely associated with, and since the 1660's the living

---

[1] Sir Egerton Brydges alleged that it was very like.

has been in the gift of, the Dean and Chapter of St. Paul's.

Then my eye lighted on the name of Etough, and the following epitaph on a monument on the south wall of the chancel:

"In memory of Henry Etough, M.A., almost 23 years Rector and faithful pastor of this parish. A firm integrity placed him above fear, and a strict love of truth above all dissimulation. His eager beneficence was tempered only by his own abilities, and the indigent merit of others. He was the warmest friend in private life, but his ruling passion was a disinterested love of the publick. With a robust constitution, through a singular habit of body, he lived many years, without the use of animal food or any fermented liquor, and died suddenly August 10th, 1757, in the 70th year of his age."

A rather pleasant, odd epitaph! But then was it possible that this could be the same person as Gray's grinning Tophet? A footnote in Clutterbuck directs one to Nichols's *Literary Anecdotes*, Vol. VIII, p. 261, "where the reader will find a long and amusing account of the eccentricities of this singular person." Accordingly, to Nichols I repaired, in the Cambridge University Library—it was appropriate to track down Etough in the very place where he had been so actively hated.

The account of the Rev. Henry Etough in Nichols is certainly amusing enough; and the numerous footnotes to the main account, the footnotes being mainly contributed by a mysterious D. M., add greatly to that interest. From the main account one learns that Etough was educated among

"Dissenters," and had "imbibed all their strongest prejudices." It is said that he hailed from Glasgow, was a
Scottish Presbyterian, was converted to the Anglican faith
and ordained. "He was principally remarkable for the
intimate knowledge of the private and domestic history of
all the great families in the kingdom. The various anecdotes
of this nature which he possessed, and which he omitted
no opportunity of communicating, made him, at the same
time, an object of outward civility and secret dislike." He
owed his preferment to Therfield in 1734 to the influence
of Sir Robert Walpole: one wonders for what services, or
whether that very great, though exceedingly cynical, Prime
Minister thought it desirable merely to conciliate a person
who possessed so many domestic secrets of great families.

According to the Rev. John Duncombe—who remembered
the rector of Therfield almost too well, owing to his frequent
pilgrimages to Cambridge—

"odd was his figure, and mean and nasty was his apparel;
his stockings were blue, darned, and coarse, and without
feet; and so hot and reeking was his head, that when he
entered a room, he often hung up his wig on a peg, and sat
bare-headed. So have I seen him."

The same authority describes him as an ecclesiastical
phenomenon, and "a most eccentric, dangerous character."
Another contemporary, a Norwich parson called Dr. Ellis,
spoke of him as a "nasty, stinking fellow, whose head was
so hot, that it used to reek like any pottage pot." But then
Dr. Ellis was himself known by contemporaries as the

238

Chapter Twenty

THE VILLAGE FÊTE

There was a time when the village of A—— enjoyed four fairs in the course of the year, by ancient grant of bygone kings: I speak of times remote, before and since the Norman Conquest. These fairs were held upon the feast days of the Annunciation of the Virgin Mary, of St. Peter, of St. James and of St. Ethelbert. To-day, only two survive, less in the form of fairs than of days of general jollity. St. Mary—to whom the church, rising with its great tower over all the countryside, is dedicated—retains her feast, not now for the Annunciation, but for the two days, early in July, nearest the Visitation. Her days are still known by the fine, round name of feast, and it is to the feast you go, not to the fair, or to the fête. Swing-boats, merry-go-rounds and sweet-stalls crammed with rock, bull's-eyes, toffee and other eminent delights in that kind, distinguish the occasion.

The second festival day which has survived is that of St. James, which comes on July 25th. But St. James, with his pilgrim's staff, scrip and escallop shell, has been wholly forgotten, and his day is now irretrievably merged in the more prosaic but universal celebration of August Bank Holiday.

It is on this day that the village fête is held, and as the village is large, we can carry off, with dignity and ease, pony and horse gymkhanas, a flower show, a poultry and what-not show, and variety entertainments provided, so the programme says, by "first-class companies of London Artistes." Among the latter the prime piece is that of "The Strongest Boy in the World," who is able to break six-inch nails, balance a man on the calf of his leg, and defy strangulation by four men with a rope. But of him more anon.

For the moment let us stroll into the large tent where the flower show is displayed. For those who are country born and bred, the hot smell of the flower tent, of fruit, roses, potatoes, humanity, mingled in an August *pot-pourri*, must ever constitute one of the lasting recollections of early childhood. I am at once seized by the ever amiable C. R., whose face is wreathed in cheerful smiles. Amid a sea of pink and purple tickets I can perceive only those bearing the triumphant name of C. R., as winner of first or second prizes for sweet peas, black currants the size of marbles, glossy potatoes, and carnations to make Perdita blush for joy.

We move next into the livestock tent—poultry, rabbits and canaries. Among these last—canaries—B., my seven-year-old son, has pulled off a second prize. But it must be confessed there were only three entries. Next door to B.'s canary a most admirable rabbit reclines lazily on his side in his small hutch. Rabbits normally sit tucked up, but this one has adopted a more original style of casual boredom, and indifferently glances at the spectators while he cleans one of his fore legs with a lazy, nibbling lick. We visit, too, the prize-winning leghorn cockerel, with his snow-white wings and scarlet comb, reared by the lame son of G., the gardener.

And now a thunderstorm, that terrible bane of all open-air festivities, descends with lightning pace upon the scene. Down comes the rain in torrents, while the thunder peals. The crowds watching the pony gymkhana rush—no, not rush, English villagers do not hurry much even for thunder: move, rather, with dignified celerity—towards the tents. As the beer tent—for the local brewery supplies refreshment on these occasions—has open sides, I move in there. The rain pours down relentlessly for a full hour. But those who attend the A—— fête are not to be lightly daunted. This has happened before. You are conscious only of an imperturbable patience. Two men behind me have improved the time and have entered the stage of genial challenge about rival dogs, their voices husky and good-natured, their horny hands clasped over some stake far exceeding the capacity of any purse that will ever be theirs. Near by, a small baby, not a year old, lies back in its pram and continuously crows with delight at the sound of the raindrops on the tent above, and the sight of the varied company sheltering within. The horses and ponies find cover with their riders, as best they can, under the trees.

But patience bears it out. The rain lessens. The clouds lift. The people emerge from the tents and stroll over the soaked grass as though it were the finest walking in the world. In the country one talks continuously about the weather; but when it comes to the point, one just ignores it.

After all, there is, among other events, a dog race to be run. This consists in running for thirty yards leading a dog, writing the owner's and dog's name on a label, tying it with a ribbon on the dog's tail, opening an umbrella, and racing home. "Ribbon to remain on dog's tail till past the post." This event is won by the ever-youthful K. W. with her satin-coated spaniel: K. W. is, to all intents and purposes, as young as her four children, of whom the eldest is seventeen.

"The Strongest Boy in the World" is now about to perform. An ample stage has been erected in the open. The crowd surges round from all quarters. A bearded manager appears, and announces that Ralleano—thrilling and appropriate name, causing a mild freezing of the blood as one pronounces it with due deliberation—is only eighteen years old. The youth appears. Gigantic indeed, six foot six, with vast chest and shoulders and herculean arms! The correspondents in *The Times* on the subject of the "manly chest" should be here. Here is no namby-pamby prudishness! Nothing but a black loin-cloth, and a vast expanse of athletic limb and torso! Ralleano moves the muscles of his arms with an elegant and easy gesture. The women in front of me give slight shudders of surprise, shock and pleased horror. See him now double up a six-inch nail as though it were a tenuous pin, and crush an apple in his palm as though it were a gooseberry!

But this is a mild prologue. He is now to lift a man with his teeth. The manager asks for a volunteer. The modest P., who has been assiduous in the beer tent, and whose innate shyness has melted away with the eighth or ninth glass, volunteers—a man of over twelve stone.

Ralleano straps him up with rope as though he were a packing-case and lays him full length upon the stage. P. lies meekly there before the gazing throng. The strongest boy in the world seizes the loose end of rope in his teeth. His muscles assume a terrible tautness. P., lying prone, log-like, immovable, nevertheless is moved, is raised, is positively suspended in mid-air by Hercules. After this, who can wonder when the matchless youth pulls a motor-car along with his teeth, and defies strangulation, four stout lads from the village hanging on to a rope round his neck (his neck protected by a towel), till the rope snaps, and Ralleano bursts his way into liberty!

At last the long day ends, the crowds disperse, and the village fête of 1932 goes with its thunderstorms, its prize carnations, its jaunty cockerels, its ponies, its excursions and alarums, its good-natured laughter, to join the beckoning ghosts of endless fêtes stretching back into dim medieval days, perhaps even into more dim Roman and pre-Roman days, far beyond the recording hand of history.

Chapter Twenty-One

ON REVISITING NORBURY

It seemed well to forget Abyssinia, and "trumpets blown for war" in Italy. And how could one forget better than by visiting again one of the most lovely country churches in all England? But there are so many that it is difficult to choose. The choice at the moment, however, was not so difficult, for we were in the neighbourhood of the river Dove in Derbyshire, and its clear water reminded one of other translucent things—as, for instance, of the exquisite chancel of Norbury Church and the knightly Fitzherberts carved in clean-cut alabaster.

I had rather forgotten the way. But a boy with an old man's face, and an expression of infinite youth, in Ashbourne directed us to the road leading out of Ashbourne towards Clifton, "and keep right on," he said, "and don't take no notice at all of turnings: it's about four miles." So right on through green country, green here despite the drought, we passed, and very soon found ourselves at Norbury with its church dedicated to St. Mary the Virgin lying a little set back from the road in entire tranquillity. Time here seems to have stopped still. You enter at a step into antiquity. The magic of it is partly explained, perhaps, by the sense, so quickly borne in upon one, of the many-centuried association of one family with Norbury. Manor houses of the early fourteenth century are extremely rare, and there, almost adjoining the west end of the church is the old home of the Fitzherberts, built, it is believed, by Sir Henry Fitzherbert, the fifth lord of Norbury, who was born sometime about the middle of the thirteenth century and died in the early part of the fourteenth. The connection of this family with Norbury goes back to 1125 and continued—despite persecution at the time following the Reformation for fidelity to the faith of their fathers—till 1649.

The nave and tower of the church—so we learn from the eminent antiquary, the Rev. J. C. Cox, whose *Notes on the Churches of Derbyshire* in four volumes are a permanent solace and source of delight—were built by Sir Nicholas Fitzherbert and his grandson John, in the second half of the fifteenth century. Pleasant they are certainly, but the glory of the church is the large chancel which was built in the middle of the fourteenth century by Henry de Kniveton, then rector and a son of another Derbyshire family of distinction. With four large windows to right and to left, and the main window in the east, the chancel is bathed in light, light transmitted partly through white, and partly through painted, glass of the fourteenth century: "there are certainly not six parish churches in the Kingdom that have so fine and extensive a display," says the learned Cox.

The eight side windows—four on each side of the chancel—contain heraldic shields beautiful with emblazonings. Apart from Fitzherbert there are—among others—the arms of Plantagenet, Clare, Beauchamp, Mowbray, Mandeville, Audley, Delamere and Montfort. So with this chime of

248

lordly names in our ears we can watch the light coming through Gules, Argent and Or, Azure and Sable. It must have been with some such recollection as this that Keats wrote of the casement in his *Eve of St. Agnes*:

> *diamonded with panes of quaint device,*
> *Innumerable of stains and splendid dyes,*
> *As are the tiger-moth's deep damask'd wings;*
> *And in the midst, 'mong thousand heraldries,*
> *And twilight saints, and dim emblazonings,*
> *A shielded scutcheon blush'd with blood of Queens and Kings,*
> *Full on this casement shone the wintry moon;*
> *And threw warm gules on Madeline's fair breast.*

The "warm gules" fall here on fifteenth-century alabaster figures of grave beauty, on Sir Nicholas Fitzherbert, tenth lord of Norbury, and on his son Sir Ralph with his wife Elizabeth: these figures lie on tombs of which the sides are finely incised with miniature carvings of the numerous children. The workmanship of these sepulchral carvings in alabaster proves to what a high point of accomplishment this typical art of midland England had come. In this medium of plastic art we can show work to compare with any in Europe: indeed, in the Middle Ages our alabaster carvings were famed on the Continent. With characteristic indifference to our own talents we have almost forgotten how eminent we were. Small figures of an angel and a monk, figures instinct with life, are carved at the feet of Nicholas and Ralph.

The inscription on Ralph's tomb has disappeared, but

a copy in the Harleian Manuscripts is given by Cox as follows:

The dart of death that no man may flee,
Nay the common lawe of mortallitie
Hath demaunded to be buried here
The body of Rafe Fitzherbert, Squiere,
Patrone of this Church and of this towen Lord:
The which deceased yeares of our Lord
One thousand four hundred eighty and three,
Of Marce the second day thus parted hee.
With him is layd upon this sepulture
Elizabeth his wyfe begun in sure
Daughter of John Marshall
Esq, Lord of Upton and of Sedsall.
Seven sonnes and eight daughters they had here
In this lyfe together whilst that they were.
Merciful Jesu that pitiest mankind,
In thy blysse graunt them a place to fynde.

The oldest monument in the Church is the noble figure of Sir Henry Fitzherbert, the fifth lord of Norbury, lying in chain armour, with his right hand clasping his sword. But with no thought of armour or swords we leave this calm place, casting a backward look at some harebells growing in the churchyard, and with an invocation for peace to "Merciful Jesu that pitiest mankind."

Chapter Twenty-Two

TRANQUILLITY

Certain words have a spell-binding power. They are all-sufficient. They convey in their compacted integrity of sound the profound experience of a state of being. Such a power there is in the word—tranquillity. Repeat it over to yourself quite slowly, and in the five seconds or so which it takes to say, you will find yourself wonderfully soothed. Moreover, calling in aid memory and the imagination, you will very soon find yourself wafted into pleasant places.

Yes! I am back there again—in the South of France, in a little sandy bay with the Mediterranean stretched before me. Azure the sky and the sea, the sun shining down in lazy brilliance, a fishing boat or two with sails the colour of crimson roses, the sand as yellow as any in *The Tempest*, pines coming down almost to the water's edge and a solitary fisherman stretched beside his beached boat, asleep. Soon I too shall be asleep, for, having bathed in that warm sea several times, and having satisfied the pangs of hunger, I have furnished myself with a bottle of golden wine. In London it would not look golden, just wan and ordinary; it is in fact very ordinary in the technical sense; but here, in the country where its fruit has ripened, it is ambrosial, an immortal nectar, sparkling in the sun. I drink this wine, relax my limbs, look up at the pines, glance once more

251

at the sea and at the sleeping fisherman, just hear the faint rippling of the serene Mediterranean in the enchanted bay, and, yes! tranquillity is lengthening its four syllables into the long river of sleep. I embark in the fisherman's boat, push off effortlessly from the shore, and find myself quite naturally gliding along the very English Cam.

So, in the twinkling of an eye, and through the faculty of dreams, late summer in the South of France has become high summer in England, in Cambridge, in the days of youth. By the Grantchester meadows, along green banks, past many a coil and recoil of the river, the canoe—the fisherman's boat has changed itself into a curved canoe—winds along. Soon G. F. will read aloud in his pleasant, quiet voice, while E. L.—it is four years before the War, and six before his golden youth will be sacrificed in the battle of the Somme—dips his paddle noiselessly in the dark waters.

It is one of the romances of William Morris that we listen to: I forget the name, but they are building an abbey-church in the fourteenth century, the masons carving the figures of the saints and many curious details in the rising walls, and somehow Margaret comes in and someone is in love with her, and before them there are great spaces of flowers. We come back to Cambridge just in time for "Hall," the emerald courts of King's placid in the evening sun, and Gibbs' Building splashed with scarlet, its window boxes being full of geraniums. The pinnacles of the chapel become more and more enormous, more serene, more clear-cut as the evening merges into night, and the moon shines down on Cambridge.

Tranquillity

I awake, for it is getting a little cold and the sun has gone down behind the pines. The fisherman, too, has roused himself and is preparing his tackle and his boat. So he launches his boat and moves over the water, and I, too, reluctantly bestir myself and leave the bay of dreams.

But not all motion is incompatible with tranquillity. Riding on horseback, rather jogging along down some green bridle-path, how tranquil that can be! For you ride out of the road, away from carts and motors and mankind. Come with me, reader, for I know a path where chicory flowers grow, and brush your stirrups and stare up with their bright blue eyes. Over a turf-covered bridge you come to a great hedge of sloes, white-blossomed in spring and purple-fruited in late summer. On by the side of a young wood of oaks, till the path becomes almost impassable with briars and over-arching hedge. The horse pushes his way through. A startled blackbird bursts from the bushes, wood pigeons take wing, and there are strange rustlings in the undergrowth. The path widens again into a grass way, the turf is firm and green, and tall elms grow on either side. Gipsies camp here, for there are burnt-out fires and tracks of caravan wheels and the tramplings of horses. And just here the bridle-path slopes sharply up hill, and after a brief climb joins a smooth, white road.

Turn back in your saddle and look at the country below you, for in these parts, from the top of any small hill you will see many a mile of England. The corn is beginning to turn: light brown, pale yellow, greenish-yellow, gold: field on field marked into a pattern of squares and oblongs,

253

large and small, stretching away and away. And here and there a small wood and the track of a road. And, most beautiful of all, the grey towers of churches rising out of the ground, murmuring benedictions, guarding their ancient villages, almost invisible among the trees.

"My soul, there is a country far beyond the stars!" The words come at once into your mind as you look at all that loveliness, and once, I will confess, I repeated Vaughan's poem aloud to my horse, and certainly he seemed to understand, as we walked home over a track through the fields.

But on a summer afternoon, in an old garden, to sit with a book! What greater peace can there be than that? In the distance you can hear the sound of the mowing of hay, and, near by, the dreamy hum of a bumble-bee as he emerges from the mouth of a snapdragon. And, better than all other country sounds, the lazy crowing of a cock, faintly answered far off by another cock after a rhythmical pause, while the summer breeze rustles the leaves, and a tortoise-shell butterfly hovers over the flowers. The sentences in the book become more and more difficult to follow, the words of a strange obscurity, the print fainter and fainter. Finally your eyes close, the mind ceases to struggle, and you fall asleep.

> O sleep! it is a gentle thing
> Beloved from pole to pole!
> To Mary-Queen the praise be given,
> She sent the gentle sleep from Heaven
> That slid into my soul.

Once, long ago, I was walking through the magnificent

aisles of Ely Cathedral. The vast pillars soared up. The great length of the nave and the enormous height of the roof, the profound stillness, the shadows and the light, filled me with an inexpressible sense of the majesty and the peace of God. I looked up and found myself standing close beside a seventeenth-century memorial. After a long recital in stately prose of the life of the deceased, all his activities, his struggles, his earthly cares, there was a single line which remains, and will ever remain, in my memory:

> "*Post Tempestatem Tranquillitas.*
> After the Storm, Peace."

INDEX

RP

Index

259

261

Index

265

Index